THIRTY DAYS WITH JESUS

Thirty Days with Jesus
*A Guide to Daily Prayer and
Contemplation on the Life of Christ*

David E. Rosage

Wipf and Stock Publishers
EUGENE, OREGON

Wipf and Stock Publishers
199 West 8th Avenue, Suite 3
Eugene, Oregon 97401

Thirty Days with Jesus
A Guide to Daily Prayer and Contemplation on the Life of Christ
By Rosage, David E.
Copyright©1990 Rosage, David E.
ISBN: 1-57910-884-9
Publication date: February, 2002
Previously published by Servant Publications, 1990.

Scripture texts in this work are taken from the New American Bible with Revised New Testament, © 1986 Confraternity of Christian Doctrine. All rights reserved. The texts from the Old Testament are taken from the New American Bible, © 1970 Confraternity of Christian Doctrine. All rights reserved. No part of the New American Bible with Revised New Testament may be reproduced without permission in writing from the copyright owner.

In Gratitude

To

my parents and family who by both word
and example launched me safely on the
pathway of prayer.

To
the teachers and spiritual directors who by
their devotion and expertise have guided
my faltering steps.

To
all the prayerful men and women I have
met in my retreat ministry who taught me
so much about prayer.

To
Mary Krone for the many hours spent in
this labor of love, preparing, editing, and
typing this manuscript.

Contents

General Introduction / ix

PART ONE: The Father's Love for Us
Introduction / xxv
1. Listening Is Praying / 1
    "Listen that you may have life..."
2. God's Creative Love / 7
    "You are precious in my eyes."
3. God's Providential Love / 13
    "Plans for your welfare and not for woe."
4. God's Reaction to the Sinfulness of the World / 17
    "How could I give you up?"
5. Is God Disappointed in Me? / 23
    "I do not do the good I want to do."
6. God's Answer to All Sin / 29
    "My love shall never leave you."

PART TWO: The Son of God Came to Save Us
Introduction / 37
7. God Prepares the Way for Our Salvation / 39
    "May it be done to me according to your word."
8. God So Loved the World / 45
    "A Savior has been born for you who is Messiah and Lord."
9. The Presentation in the Temple / 51
    "They took him to Jerusalem to present him to the Lord."
10. Jesus Begins His Public Ministry / 57
    "This is my beloved Son with whom I am well pleased."
11. The Call to Discipleship / 65
    "Come and you will see."
12. Jesus Teaches Us the Way / 71
    "Learn from me, for I am meek and humble of heart."
13. Jesus the Healer / 77
    "Your faith has saved you."
14. Who Is Jesus for Me? / 81
    "Who do you say that I am?"

15. Jesus Raises Lazarus to Life / 87
   "I am the resurrection and the life."

PART THREE: The Son Redeems Us
Introduction / 95
16. Entry Into Jerusalem / 99
   "Blessed is he who comes in the name of the Lord."
17. Jesus Gives Himself to Us in the Eucharist / 105
   "I am the bread of life."
18. Jesus' Discourse at the Last Supper / 111
   "Do not let your hearts be troubled."
19. The Agony of Jesus in the Garden / 117
   "Let this cup pass from me."
20. Trials of Jesus, Scourging, Crowning with Thorns / 121
   "He did not answer him one word."
21. Jesus Carries His Cross and Is Crucified / 127
   "Father, forgive them; they know not what they do."
22. Jesus Is Taken Down From the Cross and Laid in a Tomb / 133
   "He rolled a huge stone across the entrance of the tomb."

PART FOUR: The Risen Lord Sends the Spirit
Introduction / 141
23. The Resurrection of Jesus / 143
   "He has been raised just as he said."
24. Jesus Appears to Mary Magdalene and the Disciples / 147
   "I am the resurrection and the life."
25. The Appearance on the Road to Emmaus / 153
   "Were not our hearts burning within us?"
26. Breakfast on the Lakeshore / 159
   "Cast the net over the right side of the boat."
27. The Ascension of Jesus Into Heaven / 165
   "He was lifted up, and a cloud took him from their sight."
28. Pentecost / 169
   "They were all filled with the Holy Spirit."
29. Living With the Risen Jesus / 175
   "Remain in me, as I remain in you."
30. Finding God in All Things / 181
   "When you seek me with all your heart, you will find me with you."

General Introduction

Teach Us to Pray

One day the disciples came to Jesus with a request which pleased him very much. Jesus had just finished spending some time with the Father in prayer. Throughout his time of prayer, Jesus' whole countenance must have revealed his complete absorption in communion with the Father. The disciples might well have witnessed the peace, joy, and love which radiated on the face of Jesus.

They longed for a similar experience which would help them build an intimate, personal relationship with the Father. Their request was brief and direct: "Lord, teach us to pray" (Lk 11:1). They were unaware that this very desire to know the Father intimately was a gift from God himself. St. Paul confirms this truth when he says: "For God is the one who, for his good purpose, works in you both to desire and to work" (Phil 2:13).

Jesus was delighted to respond to their request and he did so by teaching them the Lord's Prayer. He knew that only in silent aloneness with the Father can we establish a deep personal relationship with him.

The Lord is implanting that same desire in our hearts today. We long to know God as our loving Father who abides with us and desires to love and care for us every moment. Prayer is the pathway which leads us to a love relationship with God our Father.

It is built on a simple principle. We cannot establish an intimate relationship with a person we do not know, nor can we even begin to know a person unless we communicate with and listen to that person. We must listen not merely to his or her words, but to the melody of the heart, if we would achieve intimacy.

This is equally true of our relationship with the Lord. We will come to know him with our heart as we spend time prayerfully listening to what he tells us through his Word.

Through prayer we learn to know God better, to love him more perfectly, and to serve him more faithfully. This is our whole purpose on earth. This is also the first principle and foundation of the *Spiritual Exercises of St. Ignatius* on which this prayer program is somewhat patterned.

Jesus' lifestyle confirms the necessity of prayerfully communicating with the Father. There never was, nor will there ever be, a closer relationship than Jesus had with his Father. On many occasions during his public ministry, Jesus took time to be with the Father in prayer. One such incident Mark relates in these words: "Rising very early before dawn, he left and went off to a deserted place, where he prayed" (Mk 1:35). On another occasion, Scripture says: "In those days he departed to the mountain to pray, and he spent the night in prayer to God" (Lk 6:12).

Prayer of Listening

Today in ever increasing numbers people are making that same request of Jesus: "Lord, teach us to pray." The Holy Spirit is enkindling in the hearts of his people a longing to build a more personal relationship with the Lord through prayer.

The Spirit is also inviting us to venture into a new, and for many of us, uncharted dimension of prayer—the prayer of listening, perhaps more accurately called the prayer of the heart or contemplation. For centuries, this method of prayer has been called the prayer of the heart or the prayer of listening. It is a prayer posture in which our lips and mind, our words and thoughts, come to rest. We simply gaze at the Lord letting him love us while our hearts reach out in a wordless prayer of love. It is being for God and letting God be for us. It is basking in the sunshine of his presence and letting him love us.

Contemplation cannot be adequately defined since it is an experience of God, and experiences defy definition. The great mystical work *Cloud Of Unknowing* concludes an attempt at defining contemplation with these words: "It is knowing at the core of our being that we are known and loved by God." Jesus' admonition to us might also be called a definition of contemplation. ". . . Remain in my love" (Jn 15:9). Jesus is inviting us to pray contemplatively by resting in his love, basking in the warmth and joy of knowing that we are loved and lovable.

Disposing Ourselves

Praying contemplatively is putting ourselves into the presence of God and being receptive to the love he wishes to pour out upon us. A little boy resting in the powerful arms of his father, need not say anything even if he is able to speak. He wishes only to relax and rest, to enjoy being loved and nurtured by his father. Similarly we place ourselves into the arms of our heavenly Father and simply rest there to be loved by him.

This is not easy for us since we have been influenced by the "do-er" mentality in which we live. A person is usually judged by what he or she can accomplish, rather than by whom he or she is as a person. Likewise we feel we must do something for God; we must earn his love. St. John sets the record straight when he tells us: "In this is love: not that we have loved God, but that he loved us and sent his Son as expiation for our sins" (1 Jn 4:10).

Perhaps an illustration may clarify our role and God's posture in contemplative prayer. It is like taking a sunbath. All we must do is place ourselves in the sunshine. The sun will do all the rest. It will warm us, nourish us, perhaps even burn us. Think of the sunshine as the presence or the love of God. We must place ourselves in the sunshine of his presence and permit him to do the rest.

I recall a scene that I witnessed in a two-chair barber shop. A father was sitting very quietly in one chair, and the barber did a masterful job of cutting his hair. In the other chair was his young retarded son who was restlessly squirming and trying to carry on a conversation with his father. All the other barber could do was to hold the young fellow's head and attempt to cut his hair with spotty success. As I watched this performance, I thought of it as a prayer posture. We come before God active and restless. And the Lord will not force himself upon us. He patiently waits for us to become still and quiet so that he can speak to our hearts.

Obviously, we must be quiet in mind and heart, in body and soul, in order to listen to our loving Father. Your living room or den is probably filled with radio and television signals at all hours of the day. Yet if you do not have the appropriate receiving set turned on, you will neither be able to hear the radio nor see the television picture. Likewise, we cannot "hear" the Lord unless we are attuned to his "wave length."

Prayer Posture

In a paper entitled "Simple Prayer," Sister Wendy Mary Beckett helps us understand a procedure and an attitude conducive to entering into prayer. She writes: "The essential act of prayer is to stand unprotected before God. What will he do? He will take possession of us. That he should do this is the whole purpose of life. We know we belong to God; we know, too, if we are honest, that almost despite ourselves, we keep a deathly hold on our own autonomy. We are willing, in fact, very ready to pay God lip service (just as we are ready to talk prayer rather than pray), because waving a banner keeps our conscience quiet."

This quote identifies well the benefits of listening prayer. Contemplation is a powerful method of prayer precisely because it goes beyond vocal prayer in which we verbalize our thoughts of gratitude and praise, our sorrow and petition. It even goes beyond meditation which is an intellectual reflection on some attribute of God or a scriptural revelation from which we derive insight and inspiration, enabling us to resolve to serve God more faithfully. Contemplation goes to the very reality of God, enabling us to linger in his presence, permitting him to love us and thus transform us into the kind of persons he wants us to be. In truth, all genuine prayer must have a contemplative quality.

Fruits of Contemplative Prayer

All prayer is fruitful in aiding us to draw closer to God and in bringing us to a deeper sense of gratitude and appreciation for our loving Father. Yet contemplation has a transforming power beyond our own ability. Our purpose in life is to become more Christlike, to have the image of Jesus reflected in all our attitudes and undertakings. And we become what we contemplate. When we contemplate the gentleness, the patience, and the loving concern of Jesus, we start to become like him.

St. Paul gives us the assurance of the transforming power of contemplative prayer: "All of us, gazing with unveiled face on the glory of the Lord, are being transformed into the same image from glory to glory, as from the Lord who is the Spirit" (2 Cor 3:18).

The Spirit wants us to explore the treasures of his Word in Scripture. He is urging us to let the power of that Word lead us into contemplative prayer so that we can know him experientially. Just resting in the presence of the Lord and learning to know him with our hearts—not merely with our heads—will help us form a more personal relationship with our condescending God.

Throughout my more than thirty years in the retreat ministry, I have come to appreciate the desire of so many people to know the Lord more personally and intimately as our loving Father. In this regard, vocal prayer and devotional practices, while essential and commendable, are not fulfilling the hunger which many people have for the Lord. They are searching for a greater experience of the Lord in their daily living. These dedicated people also realize that they need some guidance and support in this endeavor. The purpose of this volume is to meet, at least in part, that need.

Thirty Days with Jesus is a prayer program which offers guidance and direction for developing a mature and rich relationship with God our Father, with Jesus our Savior and Redeemer, and with the Holy Spirit our Sanctifier who teaches us how to pray. The primary focus throughout this book, however, is on Jesus, who leads us to the Father and gives us the Holy Spirit. That is why the book is entitled *Thirty Days with Jesus*. It is essentially a guide to daily prayer and contemplation on the life of Christ, which will hopefully lead you into deep listening prayer of the heart.

Several years ago Servant Publications published a book of mine entitled *Speak, Lord, Your Servant Is Listening* as a beginner's guide to scriptural prayer and meditation. The Lord has abundantly blessed that effort and has used it to bring many into a closer union with him through prayer. In a certain way, *Thirty Days with Jesus* is a sequel to that book which will lead us along a pathway, guided by God's Word, into a richer, experiential love relationship with the Lord.

Thirty Days to a Lifetime

This prayer program presents a sequence of themes which are timeless. Its thirty progressive themes provide either a thirty-day prayer experience or can be expanded into a thirty-week program by using the Scriptures provided for additional days of prayer. The themes coincide with those of the entire liturgical year in giving us a guide to prayer and contemplation on the life of Christ. In this way, the program can even extend our prayer time throughout the whole church year.

A Tested Model for Prayer

Thirty Days with Jesus is patterned somewhat on the Nineteenth Annotation Retreat of the *Spiritual Exercises of St. Ignatius*, but it does not adhere strictly to the *Spiritual Exercises*.

After his own conversion, St. Ignatius of Loyola, founder of the Society of Jesus, designed a program of spirituality which is published in a volume entitled *Spiritual Exercises*. In selecting a title, St. Ignatius was influenced by his early military career. He primarily wanted to compare a person's spiritual growth and maturation to spiritual warfare, requiring dedication and direction.

However, the book of the *Spiritual Exercises* is intended not so much for a person making a thirty-day retreat, as it is a guide and resource book for the person directing the retreatant. The *Spiritual Exercises* lists only four meditations; all the rest are contemplations. Throughout the centuries, this program has served as one of the most popular approaches to contemplative prayer.

As you follow the prayer program in *Thirty Days with Jesus,* you will discover the four sequential sections to this program, leading you from the call to follow Jesus, to the conditioning of a disciple, to a life of commitment, and then a vibrant living with the risen Jesus. The theme for each day's prayer is presented through carefully selected passages from sacred Scripture. These will serve as stepping stones leading you into the presence of the Lord in a contemplative prayer posture.

For over four hundred and fifty years the *Spiritual Exercises* have served as a challenging model for our spiritual growth, moving us from a conversion experience into a commitment to the Lord with Jesus as our ideal and model. Borrowing on this method of prayer which has withstood the test of time, *Thirty Days with Jesus* should help us climb the heights of Mt. Tabor and there to exclaim with Peter: "Lord, it is good that we are here."

Format

At first glance, the following guidelines for praying with sacred Scripture may seem too structured to permit our spirit to flow freely into prayer. However, upon further perusal, you will notice that what is recommended is really quite simple: ONE theme and ONE scriptural passage for ONE prayer period. In fact, sometimes the reader can select from one of three themes and passages for a given prayer period.

The structural approach may be compared to the setting of a precious jewel. The appropriate mounting enhances the elegance of the jewel. Likewise, the format of our prayer will add richness and depth to our experience of prayer, bringing much peace and joy to our hearts.

The themes for each prayer period are progressive and will gradually and systematically lead us into well-ordered and integrated spiritual growth. Yet love must be the motivating force calling us from a conversion into a greater commitment by treading in the footsteps of Christ. This progression may be likened to the erecting of a building, placing one brick upon another until the structure is completed. The only difference is that our structure will be completed only in heaven when we will see God face to face and will have no need to follow any more procedures.

Let us review the steps of this format which will come naturally to us as we enter this prayer time with the Lord.

Theme. Each chapter presents a different theme which will lead us step by step into the prayer of the heart.

Orientation. An orientation introduces us to the theme suggested for prayer and adds some word of explanation.

Scriptural Passage for Prayer. As we now move into the passage from Scripture, the Lord speaks to us in his Word, and he invites us to spend some time listening with our whole being to what he is trying to convey to us.

Reflections. After the scriptural passage, you will find some thoughts and reflections which hopefully will initiate and stimulate contemplative prayer.

Moving Out of Prayer. Move out of prayer slowly and gently by speaking to the Lord in a conversational manner, thanking and praising him and telling him of your love for him.

A second method is to pray slowly and reverently one of your favorite prayers, such as the Our Father.

Helpful Hints for Prayer

All the above steps are preliminary, leading us into quiet time with the Lord. At this juncture we now spend privileged time alone with him, resting in his presence, enjoying his love, being exclusively for him. The length of this period will vary, but the ideal is an hour since we need time to relax and quiet ourselves down in order to rid ourselves of all self-preoccupation and to be attentive only to the Lord.

The following "five Ps" are helpful to keep in mind during this prayer hour:

Passage. Read the scriptural passage slowly and reflectively the evening before. Let it settle into your subconscious. Read it aloud so that the message comes through two senses, sight and hearing.

Place. Select a favorite place to frequent for prayer. Having a regular place will help you get into the mood for prayer, and you will be able to enter more easily into your quiet time.

Position. Sit comfortably and erect with your feet on the floor. Concentrate on your breathing which will come more easily in this position.

Presence. Take some moments to recall that you are in the presence of the Lord and that he is happy that you have come to visit with him. Close your eyes gently and repeat your prayer word until you are quiet and receptive to whatever the Lord wishes to say to you.

A prayer word is a meaningful word or phrase which is said for a period of time, not with the lips, but with the heart, until we are relaxed and at least somewhat aware of the presence of the Lord. Such a word could be the name of "Jesus" or a short sentence or phrase like "Jesus have mercy." It can be spoken rhythmically with our breathing as we inhale and exhale.

Some people prefer a longer formula such as the Jesus Prayer, "Lord, Jesus Christ, Son of the Living God, have mercy on me a sinner."

Pray. Read the Scripture slowly and audibly, permitting each word to find a home in your heart. Recall that Christ is present in his Word and it is he himself who is speaking to you. Underline a word or phrase to which you wish to return in prayer. Let the Spirit lead you into communion with the Lord, into a time of contemplation.

Linger with that word, rest with it, savor it, taste it.

Bask in the sunshine and warmth of the Lord's love. Remain in this prayer posture as long as time permits—fifteen minutes to an hour if possible.

Use Only One Scripture for Each Prayer Time

There is a prevalent temptation that, impelled by our insatiable, intellectual curiosity, we may wish to pray at one sitting with all the scriptural passages found in each chapter, particularly with those listed at the end for additional days of prayer. But these have been added for future times of prayer. To say the least, using all of these Scriptures at one time would be a hindrance to reaching a deep experience of the prayer of the heart. Reflective reading is certainly profitable, but it will not produce the experience of God we strive for in contemplative prayer.

In trying to arrive at a deep experiential awareness of the presence of God, Scripture is only a means to an end, not an end in itself. It is a stepping stone into a union with God. The Word of God enables us to rise above our daily routine and focus more readily on some attribute or aspect of God. To achieve this end, we may not at times even need a whole scriptural passage; perhaps a single verse or a word may be enough to put us in touch with the Lord.

The maximum number of Scriptures which should be used is *one for each period of prayer*. Since this is the work of the Holy Spirit, he may even draw us back to the same passage for several days. We should remain with the lead Scripture and its reflections as long as it draws us into an awareness of the presence and love of the Lord. To wean us away from the Lord, the evil one often encourages us to flit from passage to passage, thus diverting us from entering into prayer.

In our prayer, we do not wish to obtain a superficial knowledge of various scriptural texts, but rather a deep, abiding appreciation and knowledge of the Lord and his Word. This kind of listening will transform our attitudes and our whole being.

Journaling As You Journey

Keeping a journal is an effective means for growing and maturing spiritually. A daily journal entry is a brief written account of what you experienced during your time of prayer. It is intended for your personal use only.

After your time of prayer relax for a few moments. Then review what happened while you were praying. In the form of a personal note, or even a love letter to the Lord, jot down the feelings, affections, insights, and inspirations you experienced.

At times, asking yourself some questions about your prayer may help you in journaling. Was I peaceful and quiet? Was I aware of the Lord's loving presence? Was I distracted and restless? Did the time pass quickly or slowly? It would be helpful also to note the time of your prayer and a reference to the scriptural text you used for prayer.

This reflective writing will enrich your prayer experience. It will help to foster the transformation process which began to take place within you through the power of God's Word. You may not be able to find the right words to express the experience you had in prayer; nevertheless, a few words will call to mind the whole experience in all its richness at a later date.

Keeping a journal is a form of spiritual direction. As you try to verbalize your prayer experience in writing, you will recognize more clearly the gifts, blessings, and love which the Lord has lavished on you. Your response to his love will deepen your own personal relationship with him.

A journal will also assist you in discerning God's will. Recording your experience will refine your thinking so that you may more easily recognize the direction in which the Lord is leading you. It will also make you more aware of the influences which may be sidetracking you from fulfilling God's design in your life.

Keeping a journal may seem a little burdensome at times, and the temptation will arise to neglect making an entry. However, fidelity to the practice of journaling will assure you greater growth in your union with the Lord.

The Value of Repetition

Repetition is another important step toward progress in your spiritual growth. By repetition is meant continuing your prayer on the same theme for a number of days. It can be done in two different ways.

First, you can repeat the main Scripture which was suggested in each chapter for your prayer, reviewing the reflections and insights which you enjoyed. Each Scripture passage is so rich in meaning that you can never exhaust all that the Lord is trying to convey to you.

Second, the additional passages at the end of each chapter are ideal for repeating and deepening your prayer on the theme. I have not always included more than four or five passages for a full week, because I want to encourage you to repeat even the additional Scriptures in daily prayer, rather than follow a set formula.

Using these passages for a week or more will extend your prayer into thirty weeks or even longer. You may also wish to coordinate the themes of your prayer with the liturgical season, thus extending your prayer into a year-long experience. This might mean using this book as a guide to prayer and contemplation during Advent, Christmas, Lent, and Easter.

Habit patterns are formed by repetition. Learning to type or to play the piano are only two examples of the need for repetition. The same applies to our spiritual development. If you are contemplating the patience of Jesus in dealing with his disciples or with his conniving enemies or with the little children who were brought to him, you will be forming a habit of becoming more patient in your own life without even realizing it. This is the way you will be putting on the mind and heart of Jesus.

If you repeat a prayer experience in which you enjoyed great peace, love, and joy, the repetition will increase your own sense of peace, love, and joy. On the other hand if you have experienced anger, fear, or doubt, the repetition will greatly diminish these negative feelings as you receive more of God's grace and mercy in approaching him again. This transformation and conversion process will continue as you repeat key Scriptures and themes in prayer.

A Prayer Companion or Spiritual Director

As we venture into the prayer of the heart or listening prayer, it is profitable to have a prayer companion, more commonly known as a spiritual director, with whom we can share our prayer experience. Such sharing can enrich our own life and give us a clearer understanding of God's direction.

A spiritual director assists us in discovering what God is asking of us. He or she helps us to be accountable to ourselves and to the Lord. A director is a friend and prayer companion who affirms the various manifestations of God's presence and power in our lives. His or her encouragement helps us over the rough spots which are inevitable as we progress into deeper prayer.

A director helps us discern God's will by making us sensitive to the inspirations and motivations of the Lord. The director also makes us sensitive to the tactics of the evil one who would lead us away from the Lord by creating fear, doubt, and confusion in our lives.

As mentioned earlier, keeping a journal can also be helpful in seeking spiritual direction. Therefore, you may want to review relevant portions of your journal before meeting with your spiritual director.

Check with your pastor or those on the pastoral team in your parish and solicit their advice in selecting someone as a spiritual director. You may also find it helpful to call the chancery office of your diocese and inquire about programs for spiritual direction in your area.

The Fruits of this Method

The fruits of praying with the Word of God as outlined in this book are many. In the prayer of listening, God reveals himself to our hearts as a God who loves us with an infinite, unconditional, multi-faceted love.

Unless we know him with this kind of heart knowledge, we cannot really love him, since we cannot love a person we do not know. Nor can we know a person until we have listened to him. Knowing God intellectually and theologically will engender admiration and respect, but it will not instill a mutual love.

The better we know God, the more we will love him. Furthermore, loving him will enable us to put on his mind and heart. As our love for the Lord matures, we will become more like him. In loving him, a great transformation takes place within us. We will turn away from our sinful tendencies and gradually reflect his image in our daily lives.

As this transforming process takes place within us, we will find that genuine peace which the world cannot give. Jesus told us of his love for us so that his joy might be in us and our joy may be complete. Could we ask for more?

Come before the Lord, get comfortable in his presence; and with magnanimity and humility, plead: "Lord, teach me to pray." Be assured that his gifts and graces will abound in response to your fervent prayer of the heart.

In closing, all my efforts in preparing this book for publication will be singularly blessed if they help both you and me to know the Lord better, to love him more perfectly, and to serve him more faithfully. For this, all of us can be eternally grateful.

Part One:

The Father's Love for Us

PART ONE

Introduction

AS WE ENTER INTO THIS PRAYER PROGRAM, we are confronted with two all-important questions: Who am I? and Who is God for me? Only in solitude and prayer will we find the answers to these questions. All other searching will not provide definitive answers.

I recall a man making a weekend retreat announcing when he arrived that he was seeking an answer to the same two questions: who is God and who am I? He wanted nothing less than a direct revelation from God himself. He did not receive an answer during the course of the retreat and was preparing to return home disappointed. He got into his car and turned on the ignition only to hear a booming voice say: "I am God and you are not." Whether this voice came over the radio or not has never been determined. Nonetheless, he got his answer.

Who is God?

Have you ever found yourself groping for words when a little child asks you, "Who is God?" or "What is God like?" Such an encounter is a reminder of the utter transcendence of God and our own limited comprehension of him. No vocabulary has ever been fashioned that can give us a clear intellectual image of God as the Creator and Sustainer of the entire universe, much less the God of the spirit world so far beyond our human understanding.

The inspired writers of the Bible had the same baffling problem. In the Old Testament, God manifested his presence to the Israelites at the base of Mt. Sinai as a mighty fire which caused the huge mountain to tremble (Ex 19:18). Elijah witnessed his presence on the same mountain as a "tiny whispering sound" (1 Kgs 19:12).

In the Psalms we find many images and metaphors attempting to describe some of the attributes of God. The psalmist identifies the Lord in these words, "The LORD is my shepherd..." (Ps 23). In spite of these and many other expressions, the Lord is still far beyond our human comprehension.

In the New Testament, Jesus revealed many things about the Father. Jesus taught us to call God, our Father. This image of God conjures up all the wonderful qualities of a loving, caring father for his children. Jesus assures us of the Father's infinite love for us which is manifested in his providential care and his merciful forgiveness, especially in his great desire to have us with him for all eternity.

In the quiet and solitude of listening prayer, the Lord will be able to reveal more about himself to us. This kind of prayer gives us insights far beyond our human analysis. The first section of *Thirty Days with Jesus* will lead us into a rich appreciation and a heart knowledge of the Lord. He is welcoming us into this prayer posture.

As we enter into this method of prayer and search for the answer to the question "Who is God for me?," the Lord invites us to listen that he may reveal himself more clearly to us. He is a God who loves us with a multi-faceted, infinite love.

He created us because he loves us. As creatures we are the masterpiece of God's creating love. Our bodies are the most perfect machines which were ever made. His providential love cares for us every moment. He supplies the myriad needs which keep our bodies and minds functioning all day long.

Who Am I?

As we enter into prayer with the Lord, we must honestly and humbly acknowledge who we are and our relationship to the Lord of heaven and earth. First, we must admit that we are sinners standing in need of redemption. With St. Peter we can say, "I am a sinful man" (Lk 5:8). With King David we must come before the Lord knowing that he will not spurn "a heart contrite and humbled" praying, "Have mercy on me, O God,..." (Ps 51:19, 3). Jesus also reminds us of our poverty and helplessness when he says, "... without me you can do nothing" (Jn 15:5).

In spite of our infidelities and sinfulness, our gracious God loves us anyway. The Father assures us how important we are to him: "I have called you by name: you are mine. . . . Because you are precious in my eyes and glorious, and because I love you" (Is 43:1, 4). He loves us so much he keeps us in the palm of his hand (Is 49:16).

The psalmist helps us recognize the dignity of our creatureliness when he sings, "You have made him little less than the angels, and crowned him with glory and honor" (Ps 8:6).

Baptism incorporates us into the family of God at which time the Holy Spirit makes us his special temple. In the process of adoption the Father reminds us of our dignity and his love for us: "And I will be a father to you, and you shall be sons and daughters to me" (2 Cor 6:18).

Jesus equates his love for us with the Father's love for him: "As the Father loves me, so I also love you" (Jn 15:9). Nor does Jesus abandon us in our sinfulness. He came to redeem us and he tells us, "No one has greater love than this, to lay down one's life for one's friends" (Jn 14:13).

All of the above Scriptures are convincing proofs for our intellect, but we do not live so much by our intellect as we do by our heart. We need to know deep within ourselves at the heart level who God is and who we are.

To reach this heart level and to form the attitudes which determine our reactions, we must faithfully and consistently spend time in contemplative prayer. As we listen to the Lord telling us who he is and who we are, we will come to know him and find the peace and joy which he wants us to have here in this land of exile.

This desired result will not come automatically without concerted effort on our part. In the *Spiritual Exercises* (Observation No. 5), St. Ignatius urges us to enter into this prayer experience "with magnanimity and generosity toward the Lord and to offer him ourselves entirely."

The depth of our personal relationship and love for our Father and for Jesus and for the Holy Spirit will be in direct proportion to the generosity and fidelity with which we enter into prayer.

Let us now move into prayer knowing that we are loved and lovable. The Lord bids us: "Come to me heedfully, listen, that you may have life" (Is 55:3).

ONE

Listening Is Praying

...Oh, that today you would hear his voice: "Harden not your hearts...." Ps 95:7-8

Orientation

As we begin this longer prayer experience, we would do well to realize that we are being called by the Lord to deepen our personal relationship with him through a special avenue of prayer. This kind of prayer has various names. It is called the prayer of the heart, listening prayer, or contemplation.

The Lord is inviting us to meet him in silence and solitude. We must come to him with a listening heart. Listening does not mean simply listening with our ears in the hope of hearing the Lord speak to us. Listening means putting ourselves totally into the presence of God, permitting him to inspire us, to motivate us, to encourage us, but above all to love us. It means being for God and letting him be for us. Our thoughts and words come to rest. We gaze at the Lord while our hearts respond in wordless prayer.

Prayer Posture. Listening is quietly resting, relaxing, basking in the warmth of his presence and letting him love us. It is an experience which cannot adequately be expressed in words. The author of the *Cloud Of Unknowing* tries to define it in these words: "It is knowing at the core of our being that we are known and loved by God." In only four words, Jesus not only gives us a definition, but also explains the procedure we can follow in entering this prayer of the heart: "Remain in my love" (Jn 15:9).

Listening is loving. Listening is praying. When we listen we are entering into the depths of prayer by permitting the Holy Spirit dwelling within us to penetrate our human ego and speak to our heart. Listening is then communing with the mystery of God. Quiet listening is experiencing God. Listening is not easy. We hear many things, but we seldom listen. We have learned to turn off many of the sounds which vibrate around us. We are bombarded by the telephone, television, radio, and a host of other disturbances invading our solitude and privacy.

Listening is an art. It means forgetting ourselves completely and trying to experience what the other person is feeling and the message he is trying to convey to us.

Listening Is Essential to Prayer. Listening is vital to our life of prayer. We cannot love a person we do not know, and we cannot know a person to whom we have not listened. Likewise, we cannot know God as a person unless we come to him with a listening heart.

Obviously we must be quiet in body, mind, and heart in order to listen to our gracious God. We must be open and receptive. At this very moment, the atmosphere around us is filled with radio and television signals, but we cannot hear the radio nor see the television picture unless we have the proper receiving sets. Likewise, we cannot hear the Lord unless we are attuned to his wave length.

The words of Scripture help us focus our attention on the Lord and lead us into a listening posture. However, Scripture is not an end in itself, as it would be in a Bible study. Rather it is a means of putting us in touch with the transcendent God of heaven and earth, who, in turn, draws us into a prayerful union with him.

Repeatedly throughout Scripture, the Lord invites us to meet him in his Word. God never speaks his Word without a purpose. The words of Scripture have a triple function. First, God makes known his divine truths through his Word. Second, he reveals more and more about himself, especially showing us that he is a personal, loving Father. Third, his Word establishes and enriches a loving relationship with us.

Scriptural Passage for Prayer

All you who are thirsty,
   come to the water!
You who have no money,
   come, receive grain and eat;
Come, without paying and without cost,
   drink wine and milk!
Why spend your money for what is not bread;
   your wages for what fails to satisfy?
Heed me, and you shall eat well,
   you shall delight in rich fare.
Come to me heedfully,
   listen, that you may have life.
I will renew with you the everlasting covenant,
   the benefits assured to David.
As I made him a witness to the peoples,
   a leader and commander of nations,
So shall you summon a nation you knew not,
   and nations that knew you not shall run to you,
Because of the LORD, your God,
   the Holy One of Israel, who has glorified you.
Seek the LORD while he may be found,
   call him while he is near.
Let the scoundrel forsake his way,
   and the wicked man his thoughts;
Let him turn to the LORD for mercy;
   to our God, who is generous in forgiving.
For my thoughts are not your thoughts,
   nor are your ways my ways, say the LORD.
As high as the heavens are above the earth,
   so high are my ways above your ways
   and my thoughts above your thoughts.
For just as from the heavens
   the rain and snow come down
And do not return there
   till they have watered the earth,

> making it fertile and fruitful,
> Giving seed to him who sows
>   and bread to him who eats,
> So shall my word be
>   that goes forth from my mouth;
> It shall not return to me void,
>   but shall do my will,
>   achieving the end for which I sent it.
> Yes, in joy you shall depart,
>   in peace you shall be brought back;
> Mountains and hills shall break out in song before you,
>   and all the trees of the countryside shall clap their hands.
> In place of the thornbush, the cypress shall grow,
>   instead of nettles, the myrtle.
> This shall be to the LORD's renown,
>   an everlasting imperishable sign. Is 55:1-13

Reflections

The following are a few highlights from the above passage which may stimulate your listening and resting in the Lord. Use only those thoughts which draw you into listening prayer before the Lord.

Come (vv. 1, 3)
This is an open invitation to come to the table of the Lord's Word to be sustained and nurtured. Ponder this unique invitation: the God of heaven and earth, the Sustainer and Energizer of the whole universe, wants to communicate with you. What an extraordinary privilege!

Water and bread (vv. 1-2)
Just as we require food and drink to sustain our physical existence, so his Word is essential to maintain our spiritual well-being. In his providential love, our loving Father supplies all our needs; the oxygen we breathe, the food and drink we enjoy, to mention only a few.

Come without paying and without cost, . . . (v. 1)
The only cost is our effort to be alone with the Lord in a quiet

listening posture. The Lord cannot be outdone in generosity. He will guide and direct us if we are moving toward him.

Come to me heedfully, listen that you may have life. (v. 3b)
This is the key to the prayer of the heart. Only if we are gently listening, pondering, reflecting, and remaining quiet in his presence can the Lord transform us into the kind of persons he wants us to be.

. . . the rain and snow come down. . . (v. 10)
A sufficient amount of moisture is absolutely necessary to produce a rich harvest. Likewise, the inspired Word of the Lord is vitally important for our spiritual growth and maturation.

. . . achieving the end for which I sent it. (v. 11)
"Indeed, the word of God is living and effective" (Heb 4:12). It has the potential to mold and transform our hearts and minds; our thoughts and attitudes, if we receive it prayerfully.

Joy and peace (v. 12)
When God's Word finds a home in our hearts, it will produce those special fruits of the Holy Spirit: peace and joy.

Moving Out of Prayer

Remain in prayer with the Lord as long as you can. End your prayer time gradually by praying the Our Father, slowly pausing after each phrase.

Keep a journal in which you jot down the time you spent in prayer (e.g., 7:00-7:30 A.M.), the reference of the text of Scripture you used, and some brief remarks about what happened in prayer—some insight, feeling, etc.

Texts for Additional Days of Prayer

The following scriptural passages will be helpful if you wish to pursue this theme of listening to the Lord speaking. Use only one Scripture for each day's prayer.

Matthew 11:25-30:	"Come to me ... learn from me, ..." (vv. 28-29)
Samuel 3:7-10:	... "Speak, LORD, for your servant is listening." (v. 10)
Revelation 3:14-22:	"... I stand at the door and knock." (v. 20)
Psalm 8:	"What is man that you should be mindful of him, ..." (v. 5)
Psalm 19:	"Day pours out the word to day, ..." (v. 3)
Psalm 95:	"Oh, that today you would hear his voice: ..." (v. 7)

TWO

God's Creative Love

> ... he made us, his we are;
> his people, the flock he tends. **Ps 100:3**

Orientation

Every one of us has a distinct temperament and a unique personality. However, we do have one characteristic in common. God created every one of us with a desire to love and to be loved. The desire is God's special gift to us.

We are created in the image and likeness of God and John says: "God is love" (1 Jn 4:16). God has infused this longing to love and be loved into our human nature.

This truth can also be the crux of our spiritual growth and maturation. Lurking within many of us is a fear of not being loved and even of being rejected. We recognize within ourselves so many unlovable traits. We are aware of the self-centeredness, the pride, and the ulterior motives which prompt our actions and so our self-image takes a plunge downward. We wonder how God could ever love us.

Influenced by the culture of our day, we feel that we must deserve, earn, or merit God's love. We need to know with our hearts that God loves us just as we are. God loves us unconditionally regardless of who we are or what we have done. His love doesn't change.

God's love might be compared to a brilliant light. We can remain near the light and read without any difficulty. Or we can move into the shadows of the light and be unable to see clearly. We can even close our eyes tightly and shut out the light completely. The light has not changed, but we have changed our postures. God's love is like that unchanging light; only we can put ourselves into the position to benefit from it by remaining open and receptive.

This kind of love must be translated into action. That is why God's love is active and dynamic. We can know the beauty and goodness of that love when we see it reflected in all of creation.

Look at Yourself. God created our human bodies as the most perfect machine which could ever be devised. He created our eyes with a hundred million receptors enabling us to see the majesty of his creation. That we might hear and communicate with others, our loving Father placed twenty-four thousand fibers in each ear, enabling us to pick up the manifold vibrations around us. Distributed throughout our body, the Lord has provided us with five hundred thousand touch detectors so that we can use and enjoy the myriad of objects we encounter each day. Indeed, the mystery of his creative love surrounds us.

Heart Knowledge. Reason alone will never convince us of the creating love of the Lord for each one of us. We must hear the Lord himself telling us of his boundless love. It is not enough to know intellectually; each of us must know it with our heart.

In his Word, God assures us over and over again that he created us because he loves us. We must prayerfully listen, regularly and even daily to the Lord telling us himself of his creative love, so our hearts can be convinced.

Only then in awe and reverence will we be able to respond to his love. Our response will bring us that genuine peace for which every human heart longs.

To initiate your quiet listening to the Lord telling you of his creative love, contemplate the words he spoke through the prophet Isaiah.

Scriptural Passage for Prayer

But now, thus says the LORD,
    who created you, O Jacob, and formed you, O Israel:
Fear not, for I have redeemed you;

> I have called you by name: you are mine.
> When you pass through the water, I will be with you;
> in the rivers you shall not drown.
> When you walk through fire, you shall not be burned;
> the flames shall not consume you.
> For I am the LORD, your God,
> the Holy One of Israel, your savior.
> I give Egypt as your ransom,
> Ethiopia and Seba in return for you.
> Because you are precious in my eyes
> and glorious, and because I love you.
> I give men in return for you
> and peoples in exchange for your life.
> Fear not, for I am with you;
> from the east I will bring back your descendants,
> from the west I will gather you. Is 43:1-5

Reflections

You may find a resting place in some of the following highlights.

... who created you, ... (v. 1)
Creation is an expression of love, a sharing of life. Your very existence is proof of the Lord's creative, caring love for you. Respond in your own words such as: "Thank you for loving me," or "I love you too."

... I have redeemed you, ... (v. 1)
His redemptive love conditioned us for our eternal destiny. Jesus himself said: "No one has greater love than this, to lay down one's life for one's friends" (Jn 15:13).

... I have called you by name, ... (v. 1)
In the Semitic culture, naming a child is a practice whereby the father promises to love and care for that child. Our heavenly Father assures us that he will love, cherish, and provide for all our needs. He knows each one of us by name.

... you are mine. (v. 1)
Even before our natural father could call us by name, God called

us by name. We are his. Love wants to be united with the beloved.

Water and Fire (v. 2)
Nothing is a threat to us, not even water and fire, when God's protective love overshadows us.

... you are precious... (v. 4)
What more could we ask? Only the beloved is precious.

... I love you. (v. 4)
The three most important words in our life—hear the Lord saying these words over and over again in the depth of your being. Hear him mention your own name: "_____ I love you."

... I am with you; ... (v. 5)
A lover always wants to be in the company of the person he or she loves, to enjoy, to share, to love, and be loved. God is no exception.

Moving Out of Prayer

Move out of prayer gradually by expressing your love and gratitude to God, such as "I love you, too, Lord" or "Thank you for loving me."

Making your entry in your journal is also prayer. It is a valuable tool for deeper prayer. Approach your journal with that prayerful attitude of heart.

Texts for Additional Days of Prayer

If you wish to linger for the next few days contemplating God's creative love, the following passages may prove fruitful:

Psalm 139:	"I give you thanks that I am fearfully, wonderfully made; ..." (v. 14)

Isaiah 49:1-16:	"... I will never forget you." (v. 15)
Ephesians 1:3-14:	"... for the praise of the glory of his grace that he granted us in the beloved." (v. 6)
Psalm 100:	"... he made us, his we are; ..." (v. 3)
Isaiah 40:12-31:	"... The LORD is the eternal God, creator of the ends of the earth...." (v. 28)

THREE

God's Providential Love

Only goodness and kindness follow me
all the days of my life; . . . **Ps 23:6a**

Orientation

God's love for us is so infinite that it baffles us. We cannot grasp its immensity. For this reason we try to comprehend only one or more aspects of his multifaceted love. In this prayer time, we will concentrate on God's providential love for us.

Many of us are often plagued with undue concern, worry, and anxiety about various difficulties in our lives. When these become inordinate, they overwhelm us and rob us of the peace and joy which should be ours.

The only truly effective solution to counteract these troublesome attitudes and restore and maintain our peace is a deeper awareness that the Lord loves us with a caring, concerned love. He provides for us at every moment of the day. He has meticulously planned every detail of our life and is always with us to support and encourage us.

We need to pause frequently to recall this important facet of his divine love which envelopes us at all times. Perhaps a few reflections may assist us in listening to his message, assuring us that his love is providing for us always.

Love at Work. In the last hour we have respirated over one thousand times, adding up to over twenty-five thousand times each day. God's providential love has supplied us with that priceless gift of oxygen to keep our heart beating. Every pulse beat is his gift to us, flowing forth from the inexhaustible fountain of his love.

This God-given gift of oxygen has kept our heart pulsating thirty-six million times each year, pumping six hundred thousand gallons of blood through more than sixty thousand miles of veins and arteries. This is only one manifestation of God's providing love. As we listen with our heart to what the Lord is saying to us, our appreciation of his caring, concerned love will be greatly enhanced.

A prayerful recalling of divine providence in other areas of our life will not only convince us of his boundless love, but also overwhelm us with a spirit of gratefulness. With humility and trust, we will want to respond with expressions and tokens of love and gratitude.

Jesus reminds us that his provident Father feeds the "birds in the sky" and clothes the "wild flowers." He goes on to assure us that our Father not only knows all that we need, but that he will supply each one of our needs, if only we seek his way of holiness (Mt 6:25-34).

An Ideal Prayer. That we might be ever mindful of the providential love of the Father, Jesus taught us the Lord's Prayer. In the first part of this prayer, we acknowledge and praise God as our loving Father and pray that his will might be accomplished here on earth. In the second part, we are aware of our total dependence upon his bountiful love as we implore him for all our present and future needs. We ask for our "daily bread" which includes all our spiritual and physical needs. We beg for forgiveness and redemption for past offenses. We recognize that we need his help and protection in all the trials which may challenge us in the future. The entire prayer is a reminder that God is a caring, concerned, loving Father to whom we are deeply indebted. It also calls for our trust and confidence in so gracious a Father.

Corollary. The corollary to this contemplation becomes obvious. If we grasp even in a small way that God is a caring, concerned, provident father pouring out his love upon us at every moment of the day, then there is no reason for undue anxiety. If God feeds the birds in the sky and clothes the wild flowers, Jesus asks: "will he not much more provide for you?" (Mt 6:30). A truism reminds us: "Today is the tomorrow you were worrying about yesterday, but it did not happen."

Scriptural Passage for Prayer

Speaking to us through the prophet Jeremiah, the Lord assures us of his providential love. May the many proofs of his loving concern for you find a place in your heart:

> For I know well the plans I have in mind for you, says the LORD, plans for your welfare, not for woe! plans to give you a future full of hope. When you call me, when you go to pray to me, I will listen to you. When you look for me, you will find me. Yes, when you seek me with all your heart, you will find me with you, says the LORD, and I will change your lot; . . . Jer 29:11-14a

Reflections

May some of the following comments lead you into a deeper prayer posture.

. . . I know well the plans I have in mind for you, . . . (v. 11)
God never does anything in vain. Every happening in life has a definite purpose in God's plan.

. . . plans for your welfare, . . . (v. 11)
God always brings good out of everything which happens to us, even though it may not seem likely at the time that it is taking place. Time often proves what at first seemed tragic to be a blessing.

. . . to give you a future full of hope. (v. 11)
Knowing God's love at the depth of our being increases our hope and enlivens our expectations.

. . . I will listen to you. (v. 12)
God never turns a deaf ear to our needs, nor is he ever too busy to listen. That's a divine promise.

. . . you will find me . . . (v. 13)
God is living with us and within us. We are never alone.

Moving Out of Prayer

Say the Lord's Prayer, slowly pausing after each phrase to recognize the providential love threaded throughout.

In your journal write a note of appreciation to your provident Father for his loving care and concern for you.

Texts for Additional Days of Prayer

Since repetition builds solid habit patterns, you may wish to continue listening to the Lord assuring you of his providing love.

Psalm 23:	"The LORD is my shepherd; I shall not want." (v. 1)
Matthew 6:25-34:	"Your heavenly Father knows that you need them all." (v. 32)
John 3:16:	"For God so loved the world that he gave his only Son, . . ."
John 14:21-23:	". . . we will come to him and make our dwelling with him." (v. 23)
Romans 8:28-39:	"What will separate us from the love of Christ?" (v. 35)

FOUR

God's Reaction to the Sinfulness of the World

> Wash yourselves clean! Put away your misdeeds from before my eyes; cease doing evil; learn to do good. . . . **Is 1:16-17**

Orientation

In this prayer time we emphasize the sinfulness of the world, rather than our own personal sin. Broken human nature, with all its weaknesses, has always been prone to sin and has rebelled against God who loves each of us with an unconditional love.

Sin is saying no to God. It is a refusal to love. When we love a person, we want to do whatever we can to please that person. Sin is choosing to do what our selfish human nature desires regardless of what God or others may be asking of us.

Sin is absurd and chaotic. It disrupts our whole being—our physical, psychological, spiritual life. It brings boredom, resentment, lethargy, and cynicism. It destroys interpersonal relationships and causes fear and anxiety in our lives.

We are on a journey destined for union with God himself. Sin alone can disrupt that journey and veer us away from God. Sin robs us of that peace and happiness which the Lord wants us to enjoy in this land of exile.

God is deeply disappointed in our inhumanity to each other. Motivated by greed and selfishness, we take advantage of others. We violate their human rights with impunity. We need only recall the tragedy of dysfunctional families, the pain and injustice done to the children involved, the astronomical rate of abortions in our land, or the cruel injustices done by unscrupulous persons who amass fortunes while so many starve.

We are experiencing in our society an ever increasing loss of a sense of sin. This loss has led to a growing indifference to God and his moral code. This must cause great disappointment to our loving Father who knows the misery and unhappiness which sin brings in its wake.

Our rapid and phenomenal advances in technology have made us a proud and sophisticated people. Our self-sufficiency leaves little or no room for God in our lives. He is far down on our list of priorities if he is included at all.

History repeats itself. Even a casual review of the Old Testament reveals that the rise and fall of the chosen people was directly related to their fidelity in living God's way of life.

God Loves Us Enough to Object. What is God's reaction to the sinfulness of the world? We speak of God as being angry, grieved, and outraged. These are merely representations, since we have no vocabulary to express other-worldly realities. All of the divine is beyond our comprehension.

St. Thomas Aquinas says: "God is not offended by us except in so far as we act against our own proper good" (*Contra Gentiles*, Bk. III, Ch. 22).

The purpose of this contemplation is not to dwell on the dreadful malice and horror of sin, but rather on the overwhelming love of God in spite of the malice of sin. Our focus should be on this facet of God's love—his forgiving, healing love. Yet God loves enough to object. The Lord reveals his divine pity and disappointment when he says: "I am God and not man" (Hos 11:9). His disappointment is expressed in the Good Friday liturgy taken from Micah 6:3:

"My people, my people, what have I done to you? How have I offended you? Answer me."

The Holy Spirit brings us comfort when he informs us: "Where sin increased, grace overflowed all the more" (Rom 5:20). This is the mystery of divine love.

Scriptural Passage for Prayer

The texts recommended for prayer are found mostly in the Old Testament. Human nature has not changed; hence, they are equally applicable to our times. The prophet Hosea proposes some powerful reflections for prayer:

When Israel was a child I loved him,
   out of Egypt I called my son.
The more I called them,
   the farther they went from me,
Sacrificing to the Baals
   and burning incense to idols.
Yet it was I who taught Ephraim to walk,
   who took them in my arms;
I drew them with human cords,
   with bands of love;
I fostered them like one
   who raises an infant to his cheeks;
Yet, though I stooped to feed my child,
   they did not know that I was their healer. Hos 11:1-4

How could I give you up, O Ephraim,
   or deliver you up, O Israel?
How could I treat you as Admah,
   or make you like Zeboiim?
My heart is overwhelmed,
   my pity is stirred.
I will not give vent to my blazing anger,
   I will not destroy Ephraim again;
For I am God and not man,
   the Holy One present among you;
   I will not let the flames consume you.
They shall follow the LORD,
   who roars like a lion;

When he roars,
>his sons shall come frightened from the west,
Out of Egypt they shall come trembling, like sparrows,
>from the land of Assyria, like doves;
And I will resettle them in their homes,
>says the LORD. **Hos 11:8-11**

Reflections

When Israel was a child I loved him, . . . (v. 1)
Childhood speaks to us of sinlessness and innocence.

The more I called them, . . . (v. 2)
When our self-will pursues its own course, we do not hear the Lord calling. We may even turn a deaf ear to his pleading.

I drew them with human cords, . . . (v. 4)
The Lord's limitless love cares, nurtures, and provides for us at all times in all ways.

My heart is overwhelmed, . . . (v. 8)
Love overlooks and even excuses a rebuff or a failure to respond. Love pities.

I will not give vent to my blazing anger, . . . (v. 9)
This is an anthropomorphic expression referring to God to indicate the harm we bring upon ourselves. The Lord reminds us of this when he says "For I am God not man."

I will not let the flames consume you. (v. 9)
Regardless of what we might have done, the Lord will protect us from harm.

Moving Out of Prayer

As your heart rejoices in the mystery of God's patient forbearance in spite of the sinfulness of the world, try to express in your journal your heartfelt appreciation.

Texts for Additional Days of Prayer

The following passages will be helpful for a continuing contemplation on the sinfulness of the world.

Hosea 2:4-16:	"I will lead her into the desert and speak to her heart." (v. 16)
Genesis 3:1-24:	"Why did you do such a thing?" (v. 13)
Luke 13:34-35:	"How many times I yearned to gather your children...." (v. 34)
Luke 19:41-44:	"... he saw the city and wept over it." (v. 1)

Here are some longer passages which would prove fruitful for reflective reading: Isaiah 1, Jeremiah 5, Ezekiel 16.

FIVE

Is God Disappointed in Me?

Against you only have I sinned,
and done what is evil in your sight; . . . **Ps 51:6**

Orientation

We, too, are sinners, and God is disappointed and grieved by our personal infidelities. Our sinfulness reveals our lack of faith and also how our love has lost some of its intensity. In this prayer we do not want to concentrate on a particular sin but rather on our sinfulness in general. Our sinfulness reveals itself during times when our love for God cools. We then let our selfish desires rule our conduct.

When someone we love hurts or offends us or even completely rejects us, the pain and disappointment is much greater than if a stranger did the same thing. The psalmist laments how acute was the pain when his personal and intimate friend rejected him. "If an enemy had reviled me, I could have borne it; . . . But you, my other self, my companion and my bosom friend!" (Ps 55:13-14). Jesus experienced the same painful rejection when his chosen friends denied, betrayed, and deserted him in his hour of need. Since we are the bosom friends of God, his disappointment in us must be great at times.

However, God knows our human weakness, our brokenness,

and our propensity to sin. He does not look so much at the offense as at our fundamental choice or habitual intention. If our habitual intention is always to avoid sin and obey him, God is pleased with our efforts. Even if our habitual intention is to serve God faithfully, we may, through human weakness, veer off course and sin. God does not condone these falls, but he reaches out in the compassion of his overwhelming love to bring us back on course.

God wants to forgive us so that his boundless love can be satisfied. That is why he said: "It is I, I, who wipe out, for my own sake, your offenses; your sins I remember no more" (Is 43:25). No wonder the psalmist chanted: "Happy is he whose fault is taken away, whose sin is covered" (Ps 32:1).

Shame and Confusion. Spiritual writers tell us that when we experience the infinite mercy and compassion of the Lord, it will lead us to shame and confusion. Both of these feelings are desirable and beneficial. When we experience shame, it leads us to realize more deeply that God loves us and wants to save us more than we could want it ourselves. This is a healthy attitude. We are mystified that God continues to love us and longs to forgive us, even though we fail him so frequently.

It is desirable that we try to avoid a sense of false guilt for our sinfulness. This guilt springs from pride and will lead us into sadness, depression, and discouragement.

On the other hand, if we truly love, it will lead us to genuine sorrow. Sorrow is the fruit of love. Furthermore, love more effectively deters us from sin than does the fear of guilt or punishment. Love always strives to do whatever pleases the beloved.

We need to be on our guard lest we be unduly influenced by the worldly attitudes surrounding us. To a great extent our society has lost its sense of sin. Much of the thinking of our day is materialistic. A person's worth and success in life is measured by the amount of wealth, status, power, and prestige he or she has acquired. The means of reaching these materialistic goals are often questionable, if not unjust, unethical, and even illegal. Some people live by the principle that the end justifies the means, as did one father who stole from his company in order to give his children a college education.

Greed has also been acknowledged as a national evil. This is one of the fruits of the rampant humanistic philosophy which places undue emphasis on the rights and desires of an individual while totally disregarding the rights of another person. It has been dubbed the "me, myself, and I" attitude.

We live daily in this atmosphere. Keeping our focus on the Lord will make us aware of its subtle influences and prevent us from losing our own sense of sin.

The psalmist cautions us about the possibility of gradually drifting into sin which will rob us of genuine happiness:

Happy the man who follows not
 the counsel of the wicked
Nor walks in the way of sinners,
 nor sits in the company of the insolent. Ps 1:1

Scriptural Passage for Prayer

Parables are effective teaching tools. In addition to the central message, they abound in other insights, lessons, cautions, and directives. The parable of the Rich Man and Lazarus reminds us of sins of omission.

... There was a rich man who dressed in purple garments and fine linen and dined sumptuously each day. And lying at his door was a poor man named Lazarus, covered with sores, who would gladly have eaten his fill of the scraps that fell from the rich man's table. Dogs even used to come and lick his sores. When the poor man died, he was carried away by angels to the bosom of Abraham. The rich man also died and was buried, and from the netherworld, where he was in torment, he raised his eyes and saw Abraham far off and Lazarus at his side. And he cried out, 'Father Abraham, have pity on me. Send Lazarus to dip the tip of his finger in water and cool my tongue, for I am suffering torment in these flames.' Abraham replied, 'My child, remember that you received what was good during your lifetime while Lazarus likewise received what was bad; but now he is comforted here, whereas you are tormented. Moreover, between us and you a great chasm is established to prevent anyone from crossing who might wish to go from our side to yours or from your side to ours.' He said, 'Then I beg you, father, send him to my father's house, for I have five brothers, so that he may warn them, lest they too come to this place of torment.' But Abraham replied, 'They have Moses and the prophets. Let them listen to them.' He said, 'Oh no, father Abraham, but if someone from the dead goes to them, they will repent.' Then Abraham said, 'If they will not listen to Moses and the prophets, neither will they be persuaded if someone should rise from the dead.' " Lk 16:19-31

Reflections

Make an honest review of your recent past in order to see if there has been any fault, failure, or sin of omission. Do so prudently, without concerning yourself unduly with what more you could have or might have done.

Asking yourself some personal questions may help you examine and evaluate some areas of the recent past. The following questions may help initiate such a review of your life.

Do I selfishly guard my leisure time by excusing myself on the slightest pretext when asked by someone to lend a helping hand?

Am I patient with others when they need a listening ear and an understanding heart?

Am I remiss in spending sufficient time with the Lord in quiet prayer?

Do I strive consistently to develop more fully my God-given gifts in order to serve others better?

Moving Out of Prayer

After concluding your prayer, perhaps a scriptural passage from one of the Penitential Psalms will help express your sentiments in your journal. For example, you might turn to Psalm 51.

Texts for Additional Days of Prayer

Isaiah 5:1-7:	"My friend had a vineyard..." (v. 1)
Romans 7:15-25:	"For I do not do the good I want,..." (v. 19)
Galatians 5:16-26:	"... live by the Spirit and you will certainly not gratify the desire of the flesh." (v. 16)
1 John 1:5-10; 2:1-11:	"But if anyone does sin, we have an Advocate with the Father, Jesus Christ..." (2:1)
Psalm 51:	"For I acknowledge my offense,..."(v. 5)
Psalm 32:	..."I confess my faults to the LORD,..." (v. 5)
Psalm 55:10-15:	"If an enemy had reviled me,..."(v. 13)

SIX

God's Answer to All Sin

> He pardons all your iniquities,
> he heals all your ills. **Ps 103:3**

Orientation

In our prayer, when we try to meet God in the warmth of his presence, we become painfully aware of the sinfulness of the world and our own countless infidelities. Entrenched in our human condition of continual waywardness, we cannot possibly conceive how God could love us enough to want to forgive us.

One of the gratifying dimensions of God's love is his longing to forgive and heal us every time we turn to him with a contrite heart and humble spirit. We must constantly remind ourselves that God's love is infinite. It is boundless, unconditional, unchanging.

Love must give. All love must be translated into action. If this is true of human love, how much more so is it true of divine love? Only God can forgive sin; hence, his infinite love cannot be satisfied unless he forgives.

Our Father is a God of mercy and compassion. Immediately after sin entered the Garden of Eden, God promised a Redeemer who would restore Adam and Eve's fractured relationship with himself (Gn 3:15).

At the beginning of his Gospel, John reaffirms God's redemptive love when he gives us the reason for the incarnation: "For God so loved the world that he gave his only Son, so that everyone who believes in him might not perish but might have eternal life" (Jn 3:16).

The Lord himself makes it very clear that his love prompts him to forgive when he says: "It is I, I, who wipe out, for my own sake, your offenses; your sins I remember no more" (Is 43:25). Only then will his divine love be satisfied. Julian of Norwich says:

> God waits patiently,
>   forgives absolutely,
>   forgets utterly.

Not only does God want to forgive our sinfulness, he also wants to heal us. In some cases, a certain sin is only a symptom of something that needs to be healed. For example, a person who is very unkind to another person may be acting out of insecurity or envy rather than actual malice. Perhaps he or she has permitted a resentment to fracture the relationship. The person must then be healed before this resentment becomes an impregnable wall separating the two permanently. That is why the Lord wants to heal as well as forgive us.

Joy in Forgiveness. God's question is very direct: "Do I indeed derive any pleasure from the death of the wicked? says the Lord GOD. Do I not rather rejoice when he turns from his evil way that he may live?" (Ez 18:23). As we respond to that question in our heart, there can be no doubt about God's forgiving, healing love.

There is yet another ramification to God's incomprehensible love. If we humbly and sincerely acknowledge our sinfulness to the Lord, our faults and failures can help us grow and mature spiritually. They will teach us humility and reawaken our total dependence upon God. Only divine love could bring good out of evil.

Sorrow Springs from Love. As we realize God's eagerness to forgive us when we are humbly disposed to receive his mercy, he will move us into that genuine sorrow for sin which flows from love. I vividly recall an occasion when I was doing something wrong as a youngster. My mother did not scold or punish me immediately. After some time she said: "I am glad God gave you to us." This was her way of saying that she loved me enough to forgive me. I can assure you that I thought twice before I disobeyed again.

Contemplating God's forgiving, healing love will produce similar fruits within us. The better we know and experience his love, the more difficult it will be to say no to that love. That is what sin is all about, refusing to love.

Scriptural Passage for Prayer

The Lord relays his message of ongoing forgiveness through the prophet Isaiah. As you read the passage slowly and reflectively, you may wish to underline some word or expression to which you can then return in prayer.

> For a brief moment I abandoned you,
> but with great tenderness I will take you back.
> In an outburst of wrath, for a moment
> I hid my face from you:
> But with enduring love I take pity on you,
> says the LORD, your redeemer.
> This is for me like the days of Noah,
> when I swore that the waters of Noah
> should never again deluge the earth;
> So I have sworn not to be angry with you,
> or to rebuke you.
> Though the mountains leave their place
> and the hills be shaken,
> My love shall never leave you
> nor my covenant of peace be shaken,
> says the LORD, who has mercy on you. Is 54:7-10

Reflections

The following comments are offered to enrich your prayer.

For a brief moment I abandoned you, . . . (v. 7)
When we try to describe God we must use our limited frame of

reference and speak of him as having human attributes and feelings. God could never abandon us, but this is the only way we can speak of God's disapproval of some of our actions.

... but with great tenderness I will take you back.(v. 7)
His overwhelming love brings us reassurance, peace, and joy. We realize that he is always with us regardless of what we have done.

In an outburst of wrath, ... (v. 8)
This is our human way of expressing our fear of God's refusal to forgive and our dread of punishment.

But with an enduring love I take pity on you, ... (v. 8)
This facet of God's eternal love is the source of great comfort and consolation to us, especially when we might have failed him through human sin and weakness.

Though the mountains leave their place ... (v. 10)
This is a beautiful poetic way of reinforcing the never changing love that the Lord has for us.

... who has mercy on you. (v. 10)
Our God is a God of love, mercy, and compassion. What happiness, peace, and joy should permeate our lives.

Moving Out of Prayer

Let the mystery of the Father's forgiving, healing, redeeming love sink deep within your whole being. Jot down your thoughts in your journal; let your heart speak.

Texts for Additional Days of Prayer

Listening to the Lord repeatedly assure us of his mercy, compassion, and eagerness to forgive and heal will make us grateful, peaceful persons. Here are a few suggestions:

Hosea 2:16-25:	"... I will lead her into the desert and speak to her heart." (v. 16)
Ezekiel 18:23:	"Do I indeed derive any pleasure from the death of the wicked? ..." (v. 23)
Luke 15:1-32:	"... there will be more joy in heaven over one sinner who repents ..." (v. 7)
Ephesians 2:1-10:	"But God, who is rich in mercy, because of the great love he had for us, ..."(v. 4)
Psalm 103:1-5:	"He pardons all your iniquities, he heals all your ills." (v. 40)
Psalm 32:	"... and you took away the guilt of my sin." (v. 5)

Part Two:

The Son of God Came to Save Us

PART TWO

Introduction

AS WE MOVE INTO THE SECOND PHASE of our prayer experience, our focus will be on the person of Jesus. Once again we hear Jesus ask: "Who do you say that I am?" (Mt 16:15).

In the first part, our prayer brought us to a better understanding of who God is in our lives and the accompanying awareness of who we are. It helped us recognize that we must die more fully to our selfish human nature and live more completely for the Lord.

Now, we contemplate the person of Jesus in order to become the kind of person he wants us to be. Our whole purpose in life is to become more and more like Jesus. He invites us to follow his way of life in order to reach this end: "Learn from me, for I am meek and humble of heart" (Mt 11:29).

Repeatedly, St. Paul urges us to strive for this goal of becoming Christlike. "For all of you who were baptized into Christ have clothed yourselves with Christ" (Gal 3:27). He becomes more pastoral when he admonishes us to "put on the Lord Jesus Christ" (Rom 13:14) and again, "put on the new self" (Eph 4:24).

Stepping Stones

When the first disciples met Jesus, they wondered who he was and what he was teaching. Jesus simply invited them: "Come, and you will see" (Jn 1:39). In the following Scripture recommended for your prayer time, Jesus extends the same invitation to us.

We "put on the Lord Jesus" as we listen to the words he speaks, study his attitudes, and observe his actions and reactions in his ministry. We try to experience what his heart is telling us as he reaches out to the poor and downtrodden, forgives sinners, heals the infirm, cleanses lepers, and consoles the suffering. Note the joy that fills his heart as he restores life to the son of the widow of Naim (Lk 7:11-17), sight to blind Bartimaeus (Mk 10:46-52), and promises the criminal on the cross: "Today you will be with me in Paradise" (Lk 23:39-43).

By resting in his presence with a listening heart, we come to know him better and our love for him increases accordingly. His words have the power to change us and keep our hearts in tune with his. They have the power to mold and transform us into the kind of person we are called to be. Since conversion and transformation take place in our hearts, it can happen without our even being aware of it.

To permit this process to take place, we must empty ourselves of our self-centeredness, our sinful tendencies, our frivolous ambitions, or whatever else may be preventing Jesus from filling us with his divine life and love.

The Lord's invitation is also a promise: "Come, and you will see."

SEVEN

God Prepares the Way for Our Salvation

"For he has looked upon his handmaid's lowliness; behold, from now on will all ages call me blessed." **Lk 1:48**

Orientation

As we approach the mystery of the coming of Jesus into the world as Savior and Redeemer, we begin to appreciate how meticulously God had planned every minute detail throughout salvation history. God's boundless love manifested itself in the promise of a Redeemer in the garden of Eden after sin entered the world. He reiterated that promise and gave some details of the manner of the coming of the Messiah some eight hundred years before the birth of Jesus when he said: "the virgin shall be with child, and bear a son, and shall name him Immanuel" (Is 7:14).

The immediate preparation began to unfold when God sent the angel Gabriel to announce to Mary that she was chosen to be the mother of the Messiah. All the prophecies, promises, and prayers of the Old Testament were now being fulfilled because "God so loved the world that he gave his only Son" (Jn 3:16).

St. Paul wants to bring us to a deeper appreciation of God's love for us when he explains God's desire to adopt us as his daughters and sons. "But when the fullness of time had come, God sent his

Son, born of a woman, born under the law, to ransom those under the law, so that we might receive adoption" (Gal 4:4-5).

The key person in God's divine plan is Mary, the mother of Jesus and our mother. As we pray with the scriptural account of the annunciation, we should look into the heart of Mary and try to experience what she must have felt in her mind and heart.

Model of Faith. Jesus gave us his mother as our very own because he knew that we would need a model, an ideal, if we were to live his way of life. In this episode, Mary's example of faith is a real challenge to us.

In order to appreciate Mary's great faith, we must turn back the pages of history and consider the customs of her day. Mary was asked to assume in faith the burden of tremendous responsibility.

First, it was never heard of in the annals of human history that a child could be born without a natural father. Mary was asked to accept this miraculous exception to the laws of nature. That required faith and trust.

Second, Mary was not yet married. Pregnancy outside of wedlock was not tolerated in those days. Mary was only espoused to Joseph, and such an engagement had to last for a whole year. Mary was asked to assume a great risk. She could have been rejected by Joseph, by her family, by all her own people.

Mary's tremendous faith in the face of all these odds is apparent in her reaction to the angel's request. She did not ask for time to consider the matter, nor did she ask any questions of hesitation. She requested no guarantees. Mary asked only one question and that was to ascertain more accurately the will of God in her behalf: "How can this be, since I have no relations with a man?" (Lk 1:34).

Acceptance and Confirmation. As soon as the angel explained that the Holy Spirit would come upon her and the power of the Most High would overshadow her, Mary accepted God's will in those memorable words which have come down to us throughout the centuries: "May it be done to me according to your word" (Lk 1:38).

Mary's unique faith received even more confirmation. She knew that neither Joseph nor her family would understand, but since God was miraculously working in the life of her kinswoman,

Elizabeth, she journeyed into the hill country to visit her.

As she entered the house of Zechariah, Elizabeth immediately recognized Mary's mission in life. Her acknowledgment of Mary as the mother of the Messiah confirmed Mary's own faith: "And how does this happen to me, that the mother of my Lord should come to me?" (Lk 1:43). And again: "Blessed are you who believed" (Lk 1:45).

Ask for that special grace that the gift of faith may be greatly increased in your life—that your trust in the Lord may always be without any hesitation.

Scriptural Passage for Prayer

Enter into the mystery and the sacredness of the scene as you prayerfully listen to the unfolding of God's salvific plan:

> In the sixth month, the angel Gabriel was sent from God to a town of Galilee called Nazareth, to a virgin betrothed to a man named Joseph, of the house of David, and the virgin's name was Mary. And coming to her, he said, "Hail, favored one! The Lord is with you." But she was greatly troubled at what was said and pondered what sort of greeting this might be. Then the angel said to her, "Do not be afraid, Mary, for you have found favor with God. Behold, you will conceive in your womb and bear a son, and you shall name him Jesus. He will be great and will be called Son of the Most High, and the Lord God will give him the throne of David his father, and he will rule over the house of Jacob forever, and of his kingdom there will be no end." But Mary said to the angel, "How can this be, since I have no relations with a man?" And the angel said to her in reply, "The holy Spirit will come upon you, and the power of the Most High will overshadow you. Therefore the child to be born will be called holy, the Son of God. And behold, Elizabeth, your relative, has also conceived a son in her old age, and this is the sixth month for her who was called barren; for nothing will be impossible for God." Mary said, "Behold, I am the handmaid of the Lord. May it be done to me according to your word." Then the angel departed from her. Lk 1:26-38

Reflections

These comments will hopefully serve as stepping stones into a deeper prayer experience. Let the Spirit lead you in his own inimitable way.

... "Hail, favored one!" (v. 28)
This was a unique greeting and it startled Mary, especially because of the appearance of an angel.

But she was greatly troubled ... (v. 29)
In all her humility Mary would never expect to be honored by such a visitor.

... "Do not be afraid, ..." (v. 30)
Throughout Scripture when God is at work, it inspires fear, awe, and reverence. In every instance the person is reassured and encouraged not to be afraid.

"... He will be great and will be called Son of the Most High, ..." (v. 32)
What a startling message this must have been for Mary! Such a divine presence was unheard of.

"... the power of the Most High will overshadow you. ..." (v. 35)
Since Mary was sinless, she was already the temple of the Holy Spirit who was operative and dynamic within her. The Spirit had already strengthened her faith as she matured in his presence.

... "Behold, I am the handmaid of the Lord. ..." (v. 38)
This total gift of herself to the Lord was most pleasing to him. Mary's great humility is reflected in this statement.

"... May it be done to me according to your word." (v. 38)
This was a perfect oblation of herself to God. Mary never reneged on that commitment, not even under the shadow of the cross.

Moving Out of Prayer

Pray the Hail Mary slowly and thoughtfully. Then write Mary a brief note of admiration and gratitude in your journal.

Texts for Additional Days of Prayer

To enter more deeply into this mystery of God's salvific plan, you may wish to reflect on some additional scriptural passages. They will bring you into deeper, richer appreciation of God's redemptive love.

Luke 1:39-56:	"And how does this happen to me, that the mother of my Lord should come to me?" (v. 43)
Matthew 1:18-25:	"Joseph, son of David, do not be afraid to take Mary your wife into your home." (v. 20)
Galatians 4:1-7:	". . . God sent his Son, born of a woman, . . ." (v. 4)
Psalm 33:	"From heaven the LORD looks down; . . ." (v. 13)

EIGHT

God So Loved the World

And the Word became flesh and made his dwelling among us, and we saw his glory, the glory as of the Father's only Son, full of grace and truth. Jn 1:14

Orientation

The Christmas season is a time of celebration and rejoicing. We send messages of peace and joy to family and friends. We express our gratitude and love for one another by sharing gifts. There are joyous greetings ringing out as friend meets friend, even as stranger meets stranger. The whole world seems to pause in its hustle and bustle to celebrate the birth of Jesus.

Love. The reason for this universal jubilation is not simply the anniversary of Jesus' birth. It is a response to the mystery of God's tremendous love manifested in this annual event.

The human race severed its relationship with God by refusing to obey his will in the Garden of Eden. God could have abandoned his creatures at that time, but his love prevailed. "For God so loved the world that he gave his only Son, so that everyone who believes in him might not perish but might have eternal life" (Jn 3:16). The coming of Jesus as Savior rekindled the hope that had endured throughout the ages. A committed faith in him is a guarantee that we "might have eternal life," fulfilling this hope which has still prevailed throughout the centuries. Knowing that we are so loved by God is a sufficient cause for rejoicing.

Fidelity. As one of the greatest events in human history, the incarnation reveals the fidelity of God to his promises. In the Garden, he already promised a Redeemer when he assured us that the power of the devil would be broken. "I will put enmity between you and the woman, and between your offspring and hers; He will strike at your head, while you strike at his heel" (Gn 3:15). As the offspring of the woman, Jesus conquered sin and death by breaking the power of the evil one.

Throughout the long centuries of waiting, the Lord repeated his promises in more detail and with greater clarity. Bethlehem was the beginning of the fulfillment of all these divine promises. A prayerful recalling of God's enduring fidelity can be the source of much joy in our life.

Peace. Within the heart of every human being, there is a longing for some kind of fulfillment—a desire for genuine peace. As foretold by the prophets, Jesus came into the world as the "Prince of Peace." He bequeathed that peace to us at the solemn moment of his earthly sojourn. In his final discourse in the Upper Room, the night before he died, Jesus promised: "Peace I leave with you; my peace I give to you" (Jn 14:27).

The kind of peace which Jesus promised, and for which we are all striving, is the fruit of good wholesome relationships on four levels: with God as our Father, with ourselves, with our neighbor, and with all of creation.

Jesus gained that peace for us by his passion and death. It is now dispensed to us as the fruit of the Holy Spirit. "The fruit of the Spirit is love, joy, peace . . ." (Gal 5:22). Experiencing this God-given gift of peace is another reason for rejoicing at the Christmas season and all the days of our life.

God's Way. The Father sent his Son into our broken world as a helpless, vulnerable child in order to win our love. Had he come as a mighty warrior or a dynamic political leader, or a great revivalist, we might have feared the consequences of not accepting him. The

Lord asks only our loving acceptance and our loyalty arising out of love.

The angels delivered a powerful message to us. It is a two-pronged directive. Our first duty is to give God glory and honor. Second, we are to live his way of life so that we may enjoy the peace he wishes to give us. The angels sang:

> "Glory to God in the highest
> and on earth peace to those on whom
> his favor rests."

We give God glory and praise because Jesus, being born eucharistically every day, makes every day Christmas.

Scriptural Passage for Prayer

We are very familiar with the Gospel story of the birth of Jesus. For this reason, we may hesitate to use it as the source of our prayer. If such thoughts come to mind, we can be certain that there is always something new and challenging in the Word of God. Thomas Merton says: "Contemplation gives us insights beyond analysis." Mindful of this truth, let us explore the mystery of God's love:

> In those days a decree went out from Caesar Augustus that the whole world should be enrolled. This was the first enrollment, when Quirinius was governor of Syria. So all went to be enrolled, each to his own town. And Joseph too went up from Galilee from the town of Nazareth to Judea, to the city of David that is called Bethlehem, because he was of the house and family of David, to be enrolled with Mary, his betrothed, who was with child. While they were there, the time came for her to have her child, and she gave birth to her firstborn son. She wrapped him in swaddling clothes and laid him in a manger, because there was no room for them in the inn.
>
> Now there were shepherds in that region living in the fields and keeping the night watch over their flock. The angel of the Lord appeared to them and the glory of the Lord shone around them, and they were struck with great fear. The angel said to

them, "Do not be afraid; for behold, I proclaim to you good news of great joy that will be for all the people. For today in the city of David a savior has been born for you who is Messiah and Lord. And this will be a sign for you: you will find an infant wrapped in swaddling clothes and lying in a manger." And suddenly there was a multitude of the heavenly host with the angel, praising God and saying:

"Glory to God in the highest
and on earth peace to those on whom his favor rests."

When the angels went away from them to heaven, the shepherds said to one another, "Let us go, then, to Bethlehem to see this thing that has taken place, which the Lord has made known to us." So they went in haste and found Mary and Joseph, and the infant lying in the manger. When they saw this, they made known the message that had been told them about this child. All who heard it were amazed by what had been told them by the shepherds. And Mary kept all these things, reflecting on them in her heart. Then the shepherds returned, glorifying and praising God for all they had heard and seen, just as it had been told to them. Lk 2:1-20

Reflections

Some of the following comments may lead us into prayer as we listen to the Lord's joyful message.

... laid him in a manger, ... (v. 7)
St. Luke uses a great deal of symbolism in the nativity narratives. Mangers were hollowed out rock and used for feeding livestock. Jesus was laid in a manger to symbolize that he was going to feed us down through the ages.

"... For today in the city of David a savior has been born for you who is Messiah and Lord...." (v. 11)
In this single sentence we discover the mission of Jesus. He came to save the world; he is the promised Redeemer and Lord of all creation.

So they went in haste ... (v. 16)
The shepherds were men of faith. They believed the message of

the angel and set out to find the infant. They understood who he was and immediately began to make "known the message that had been told them about the child."

And Mary kept all these things, reflecting on them in her heart. (v. 19)
Surely Mary could not understand the workings of the Lord in the shepherds; hence, she went into prayer to reflect on the Lord's mysterious workings.

Then the shepherds returned, glorifying and praising God . . . (v. 20)
May the limitless dimensions of God's love which we discover in prayer keep us praising and glorifying God also.

Moving Out of Prayer

After humming a Christmas hymn to yourself, in spirit kneel at the crib in Bethlehem and write in your journal whatever is in your heart.

Texts for Additional Days of Prayer

If you wish to explore other dimensions of this great event in human history, you may find some of the following texts rewarding.

John 1:1-18:	"And the Word became flesh and made his dwelling among us, . . ." (v. 14)
Colossians 1:15-20:	"For in him were created all things in heaven and on earth, . . ." (v. 16)
1 John 1:1-4:	". . . what we have seen and heard we proclaim now to you, . . ." (v. 3)
Wisdom 18:14-16:	"Your all-powerful word from heaven's royal throne bounded, . . . into the doomed land." (v. 15)
Galatians 4:1-7:	"But when the fullness of time had come God sent his Son, born of a woman, . . ." (v. 4)

NINE

The Presentation in the Temple

> ... And suddenly there will come to the
> temple the LORD whom you seek,
> And the messenger of the covenant whom
> you desire.... **Mal 3:1**

Introduction

The theme for this prayer of listening is presented in three separate sections, since these closely related events took place in the temple in rapid succession. May the Holy Spirit direct you to one or all of these separate accounts as the source of your prayer.

The Presentation

> ... And suddenly there will come to the temple
> the LORD whom you seek,
> And the messenger of the covenant whom you desire....
> **Mal 3:1**

Orientation. Accompany Mary and Joseph as they make the six-mile journey from Bethlehem to Jerusalem to present the Child Jesus to the Lord as prescribed by the law. Even though they were exempt from the law, nevertheless, they were willing to obey its prescripts.

We can well imagine that they were delighted to show their infant to everyone who stopped along the way to admire him. In all humility they must have kept the secret of his identity locked in their own hearts as the Spirit led them. As you listen to the words of Scripture, let your heart read between the lines.

Scriptural Passage for Prayer.

> When the days were completed for their purification according to the law of Moses, they took him up to Jerusalem to present him to the Lord, just as it is written in the law of the Lord, "Every male that opens the womb shall be consecrated to the Lord," and to offer the sacrifice of "a pair of turtledoves or two young pigeons," in accordance with the dictate in the law of the Lord. **Lk 2:22-24**

Reflections. The Scripture passage for this prayer period can be naturally divided into three sections, all of which took place at the presentation of Jesus in the temple. Since the Holy Spirit not only draws us into prayer, but also prays within us, the usual specific suggestions have not been made under the heading of Reflections. Instead some general thoughts follow with the hope that your spirit will be more open to the inspirations and insights of the Holy Spirit.

> **Note to reader: This more general approach is taken in these "Reflections" sections at various points throughout this book. Where such is the case, you are encouraged to use your imagination and to be more open to the inspiration of the Holy Spirit.**

The hearts of Mary and Joseph must have been filled with joy as they gradually began to realize that the redemption of Israel was approaching. Likewise, their minds and hearts were in tune with the will of the Lord and they were happy to make this oblation of their Son.

Our daily offering of ourselves and all that we do to the Lord will bring us genuine peace and great satisfaction. The "Morning Offering" in union with the Immaculate Heart of Mary, along with every Mass which is being offered, is an ideal method of making our own daily presentation to God.

Mary and Joseph were happy to make the offering of the poor, "a pair of turtledoves or two young pigeons." Their poverty was no embarrassment to them. It helped them, as it does us, to remain detached from worldly concerns in order to keep our focus more readily on the Lord.

Even though their Son was the Lord of the law, they did not claim any exemption from the law, but fulfilled every detail of the law of Moses. This manifested their poverty of spirit as well as their material poverty.

Simeon's Prophecy

Orientation. Luke's account of the presentation in the temple continues with another extraordinary event planned by God. Simeon, responding to the promptings of the Spirit, came into the temple at this precise time to meet the Holy Family. Let the inspired words of the Gospel enlighten you with the richness and meaning of this event.

Scriptural Passage for Prayer.

Now there was a man in Jerusalem whose name was Simeon. This man was righteous and devout, awaiting the consolation of Israel, and the holy Spirit was upon him. It had been revealed to him by the holy Spirit that he should not see death before he had seen the Messiah of the Lord. He came in the Spirit into the temple; and when the parents brought in the child Jesus to perform the custom of the law in regard to him, he took him into his arms and blessed God, saying:

"Now, Master, you may let your servant go
   in peace, according to your word,
for my eyes have seen your salvation,
   which you prepared in sight of all the peoples,
a light for revelation to the Gentiles,
   and glory for your people Israel."

The child's father and mother were amazed at what was said about him; and Simeon blessed them and said to Mary his mother, "Behold, this child is destined for the fall and rise of many in Israel, and to be a sign that will be contradicted (and you yourself a sword will pierce) so that the thoughts of many hearts may be revealed." **Lk 2:25-35**

Reflections. Simeon was "righteous and devout" which made him receptive and docile to the inspirations of the Holy Spirit. Living his life above reproach enabled the Holy Spirit to endow him with a strong, dynamic faith that matured with the passing of the years. His heart was always attuned to the influence and grace of the Spirit. Simeon's openness and cooperation enabled the Holy Spirit to enlighten him about the salvific plan of God. Thus, he was able to recognize the babe in the arms of Mary as the "Messiah of the Lord."

As we endeavor to avoid sin in our lives, the Holy Spirit can more effectively transform us and fill us with his divine gifts. Time spent in prayer will bring us wisdom and understanding beyond human comprehension.

Simeon's prophetic vision of the rejection of Jesus as "a sign that will be contradicted" and the pain and suffering which would be involved in his redemptive mission, prepared Mary and Joseph for the unfolding of the Father's mysterious plan for the redemption of the human race.

"The child's father and mother were amazed at what was said about him." Mary and Joseph must have been surprised that Simeon recognized their child as the long-awaited Savior of the world. This prophetic revelation readily raised their minds and hearts to praise God for the marvels of his plan. Have we not experienced wonders in our own life?

Anna's Testimony

Orientation. As the God of surprises, he has yet another wonder in store for the Holy Family and us. Another prophetic vision was to unfold as Anna recognized and acknowledged Jesus as the promised Messiah. Luke's account may seem brief, but its mystery fills us with awe and reverence. Listen:

Scriptural Passage for Prayer.

There was also a prophetess, Anna, the daughter of Phanuel, of the tribe of Asher. She was advanced in years, having lived seven years with her husband after her marriage, and then as a widow until she was eighty-four. She never left the temple, but worshiped night and day with fasting and prayer. And coming forward at that very time, she gave thanks to God and spoke about the child to all who were awaiting the redemption of Jerusalem. Lk 2:36-38

Reflections. Anna gives us the key to an intimate, personal union with God: she "worshiped night and day with fasting and prayer." Fasting is much more than merely a penitential discipline, it is a means of leading us into prayer. It helps us to remove ourselves from worldly demands and distractions so we can focus on our loving Father. Fasting is the one discipline mentioned repeatedly throughout the Scriptures.

Anna was a woman of prayer. Prayer builds our relationship with God. As a building is erected brick upon brick, likewise our daily time in prayer establishes and enriches our relationship with the Lord.

Anna became one of the first bearers of the good news as she "spoke about the child to all who were awaiting the redemption of Jerusalem." Her own lifestyle added great credibility to the message she was proclaiming.

As we contemplate these scenes, our hearts will be filled with gratitude to the Lord for the inspiration and encouragement gained from each person involved in the presentation. May our lives always give such witness to the goodness of the Lord.

Moving Out of Prayer

In your closing prayer rededicate yourself to the Lord. The gift of ourselves is all that he asks. You may wish to record the offering of yourself in your journal.

Texts for Additional Days of Prayer

There are other events recorded in Scripture about the birth of Jesus which you may wish to use for continued prayer.

Matthew 2:1-12:	The Visit of the Magi—The committed faith and determined perseverance of the wise men challenges us to emulate their example.
Matthew 2:13-15:	The Flight to Egypt—The rejection of Jesus as prophesied not only by Simeon, but by many other prophets in the Old Testament, was beginning to be fulfilled.
Matthew 2:16-18:	The Massacre of the Infants—The depravity of Herod was indicative of the many down through the centuries who would persecute the followers of Jesus. Martyrdom still goes on.
1 Samuel 2:1-11:	"My heart exults in the Lord, my horn is exalted in my God...." (v. 1)
2 Maccabees 7:20-42:	"Most admirable and worthy of lasting remembrance was the mother, who saw her seven sons perish in a single day." (v. 20)

TEN

Jesus Begins His Public Ministry

Introduction

At this point in the evolving themes for our prayer, we are contemplating three closely related events in the life of Jesus. These events are related chronologically as they follow each one in rapid sequence. They are also related because they are the steps which launched Jesus into his public ministry. They are further related since we experience similar stages in our Christian vocation and ministry—our call, conditioning, and commitment.

As we reach this stage in our prayer life, St. Ignatius proposes a meditation on what he calls the "Two Standards." The first is the standard of the evil one. Knowing the weakness of our broken human nature, the devil entices us to follow him by deceitfully offering us riches, honor and pride.

The standard of Jesus is diametrically opposed to that of Satan. Jesus is honest in telling us what he is offering us if we follow him: poverty as opposed to riches; insults and contempt as opposed to the empty honors of the world; and humility as opposed to pride. This is the time of decision.

In the following prayer periods, Jesus shows us the way as he leaves home to begin his public ministry; even though sinless, he submits to the penitential rite of baptism by John in the Jordan and permits the devil to tempt him in the desert.

Jesus Leaves Home

> ... Jesus came from Nazareth of Galilee and was baptized in the Jordan by John. **Mk 1:9**

Orientation. Visit Nazareth and try to experience the pain of separation which Jesus and Mary both suffered. This parting is so sacred that Scripture hesitates to mention it. There is only one oblique reference to it: "It happened in those days that Jesus came from Nazareth of Galilee and was baptized in the Jordan by John" (Mk 1:9).

We can well visualize Mary walking with her Son to the edge of the village of Nazareth and standing there watching him walk eastward toward the Jordan until he disappeared from view. We can surely sense the emptiness in Mary's heart.

Walk with Jesus as he journeys toward the Jordan. Words cannot convey his feelings. Silence speaks eloquently. In prayer, try to experience what life would be like without Jesus. Thank him for abiding always with you and within you.

Note to reader: There are no Scriptures and reflections on this event since it is not recorded in the Bible. Let your imagination in prayer guide you into a time of contemplation.

Baptism of Jesus

Orientation. Jesus humbly submitted to this penitential rite of baptism to set an example for us by pointing out our need for repentance and forgiveness. Jesus was sinless, but he assumed the burden of our sinfulness, "nailing it to the cross" (Col 2:14).

This was the first theophany to take place in the New Testament. It clearly manifests the presence of the Holy Trinity— Father, Son, and Holy Spirit. Since Jesus was now launching forth on his mission of proclaiming the good news, the Father's voice gave him an unqualified endorsement for the benefit of the bystanders: "This is my beloved Son, with whom I am well pleased." With the Spirit descending like a dove, we become more fully aware that the work of redemption is the work of the whole Godhead.

Scriptural Passage for Prayer.

> Then Jesus came from Galilee to John at the Jordan to be baptized by him. John tried to prevent him, saying, "I need to be baptized by you, and yet you are coming to me?" Jesus said to him in reply, "Allow it now, for thus it is fitting for us to fulfill all righteousness." Then he allowed him. After Jesus was baptized, he came up from the water and behold, the heavens were opened [for him], and he saw the Spirit of God descending like a dove [and] coming upon him. And a voice came from the heavens, saying, "This is my beloved Son, with whom I am well pleased." Mt 3:13-17

Reflections. No specific or detailed reflections are given here in order to give the pray-er an opportunity to have a personal faith experience. As you contemplate this scene, you may wish to converse with Jesus asking him how he felt as he presented himself for this penitential rite. Was he happy to see his kinsman? Was he pleased to see the number of people who came out to hear the message of John the Baptizer? Was he eager to begin his public ministry? What other thoughts and feelings might he have had?

In your prayer try to see yourself present at the Jordan, as if you could *hear* the *murmur* of the crowd or even *touch* the water to feel how *warm* or *cold* it might be. *Sit quietly* on the bank of the river and *listen intently* as the Father makes his solemn pronouncement about Jesus.

As you rest in prayer, try to realize that the Blessed Trinity is present to you. You are resting in God's presence. Hear the Father say to you: "Listen to my Son."

Luke adds an encouraging detail to his account of the baptism of Jesus. After "Jesus also had been baptized and was praying, heaven was opened" (Lk 3:21). It is in prayer that heaven will also open to us.

Jesus Tempted in the Desert

Orientation. The temptation of Jesus was primarily an inner struggle to determine how he was to carry on his mission of evangelizing the world. It was a testing of his motives and the methods he was to employ. It was a struggle in his own mind, heart, and soul. His inmost thoughts and desires had to be tested to ascertain more accurately the Father's plan for him.

We know about this battle which Jesus faced only because Jesus himself must have revealed it to his followers, and therefore to us in his Word. He was preparing them and us for similar struggles in fulfilling our mission in life.

The central theme in this testing experience of Jesus was the temptation to turn from carrying out his mission according to the will of the Father and choose another course which would be more fruitful. The devil tried to give credence to his allurements by even quoting Scripture. Jesus refuted him by quoting other Scriptures to the contrary.

The tempter encouraged Jesus to turn stones into bread because he was hungry. Further, he could bribe the people to follow him by giving them bread without cost. Jesus' rebuttal was right to the point: "One does not live by bread alone . . ." Jesus never used his divine power for any selfish reason.

The second temptation was of a similar nature. It proposed that Jesus stand on the parapet of the temple where the priests stood every morning announcing the beginning of a new day. If Jesus plunged some four hundred and fifty feet into the Kedron Valley below without injury, it would have been a sensational feat. People would have followed him in droves. Jesus resisted the thought by recalling another passage from Scripture: "You shall not put the Lord, your God, to the test."

The third test was an invitation to compromise. Do not preach the Word that the Lord alone is to be worshiped, but make the message more palpable. Give them something that will appeal to the whole world, and your followers will be many. Once again Jesus conquered this temptation with the reminder: "The Lord, your God, shall you worship and him alone shall you serve."

Jesus made a firm decision. He would never try to bribe anyone to follow him, nor would he use any sensational method to encourage followers to come to him, nor would he ever compromise the message he was sent to proclaim. He asked only for a deep, committed faith. Jesus was aware that this choice would inevitably lead to the cross, but that cross would be his final victory and his glorification.

Scriptural Passage for Prayer. Listen prayerfully and appreciatively as this struggle and decision is presented in the Gospel:

> Then Jesus was led by the Spirit into the desert to be tempted by the devil. He fasted for forty days and forty nights, and afterwards he was hungry. The tempter approached and said to him, "If you are the Son of God, command that these stones become loaves of bread." He said in reply, "It is written: 'One does not live by bread alone, but by every word that comes forth from the mouth of God.'" Then the devil took him to the holy city, and made him stand on the parapet of the temple, and said to him, "If you are the Son of God, throw yourself down. For it is written: 'He will command his angels concerning you,' and 'with their hands they will support you, lest you dash your foot against a stone.'" Jesus answered him, "Again it is written, 'You shall not put the Lord, your God, to the test.'" Then the devil took him up to a very high mountain, and showed him all the kingdoms of the world in their magnificence, and he said to him, "All these I shall give to you, if you will prostrate yourself and worship me." At this, Jesus said to him, "Get away, Satan! It is written: 'The Lord, your God, shall you worship and him alone shall you serve.'"
>
> Then the devil left him and, behold, angels came and ministered to him. Mt 4:1-11

Reflections.

... led by the Spirit ... (v. 1)
The Holy Spirit will permit us to be tempted in order to strengthen us against falling into sin. Temptations will also enable us to grow and mature spiritually.

... into the desert ... (v. 1)
Jesus was all alone which points to his inner struggle. Our special gifts will often be the source of our temptation. In our own heart we must resolve to use temptations for the honor and glory of God and in the manner God wills.

He fasted for forty days and forty nights, ... (v. 2)
Fasting is not only a penitential discipline, but also a means of leading us into deeper prayer.

"... 'One does not live by bread alone, ...'" (v. 4)
In the Gospel the word "bread" is often used to include all God's gifts: faith in his Word, etc.

"... 'You shall not put the Lord, your God, to the test.'" (v. 7)
Jesus gave us the example by not succumbing to the temptation of using any means to win followers, but adhered strictly to the mission as planned by his Father. There is a great lesson contained therein.

"... 'The Lord, your God, shall you worship and him alone shall you serve.'" (v. 10)
Doing everything according to the will of the Lord is the best way of serving God, our neighbor, and ourselves.

Moving Out of Prayer

Along with your concluding prayer, journaling is a powerful means for growing and maturing in your personal relationship with the Lord. Consider how you have grown in that relationship through this time of prayer and contemplation.

Texts for Additional Days of Prayer

There are parallel passages of the baptism and temptation of Jesus in Mark 1:9-13, Luke 3:21-22, and Luke 4:1-13 which might afford some different insights into these events.

Other passages which will enable you to live closely to Jesus as he struggles with his mission are:

Philippians 2:5-11:	"Rather, he emptied himself, taking the form of a slave, coming in human likeness;..." (v. 7)
Hebrews 2:5-18:	"Because he himself was tested through what he suffered, he is able to help those who are being tested." (v. 18)

ELEVEN

The Call to Discipleship

> ... He said to him, "Follow me." And he got up and followed him. **Mt 9:9**

Orientation

In the *Spiritual Exercises*, St. Ignatius urges us to spend time contemplating the Lord's invitation to come follow him. He headlines this prayer time as the "Call of the King."

Throughout the ages many great and gifted leaders have arisen who have advocated a particular cause and pleaded for followers to join them in their special crusade. They did not hesitate to encourage their followers to sacrifice time, talent, and treasure to achieve a designated goal which was usually rather worldly and at times even evil.

Come Follow Me. Jesus came into the world to establish his reign as a spiritual king. As king of heaven and earth, he invites us to follow his way of life so that we might enjoy eternal happiness in his kingdom forever. He wants us to follow him so closely that we can be identified with him. He calls us to become his disciples. A disciple constantly observes the master so that eventually he will think, speak, and react like the master. This is the import of Jesus' request: "Learn from me, for I am meek and humble of heart" (Mt 11:29).

Know Jesus. We cannot become like Jesus unless we know him. The only way that we really know Jesus as a person is by meeting him in the prayer of the heart—listening at the depth of our being as he reveals his mind and heart to us. As we encounter Jesus in this way, we discover that he is single-minded in doing exactly what the Father wills. This facet of Jesus' personality automatically urges us to become like him by determining exactly what the Father desires of us in any given situation.

In order for us to stay in tune with the will of God, Jesus tells us that we must be motivated by love: "You shall love the Lord, your God, with all your heart, with all your being, with all your strength, and with all your mind, and your neighbor as yourself" (Lk 10:27). We cannot love a person unless we know that person.

Key to Knowing Jesus. (a) We must desire to know Jesus with all our heart by continually asking for the grace to deepen our personal relationship with him. Jesus wants to establish a more intimate relationship with us, but he never forces himself upon us. He waits for us to ask and to be open and receive him.

(b) We must relate to the humanity of Jesus. We can more easily identify with the Jesus who gets hungry and thirsty, who hugs lepers, who eats with sinners and tax collectors, who is lovingly concerned about lepers and the outcasts, who weeps at the loss of a friend, who loves his enemies, who lays down his life for us.

(c) We must strive to imitate Jesus' attitudes and actions: his love for the poor and downtrodden, his loving concern for the sick and suffering, his eagerness to forgive, his zeal in proclaiming the good news.

(d) We get to know Jesus by applying our senses: observing the persons in the various Gospel scenes, listening to what is being said, imagining the personalities of the persons involved, focusing on what Jesus is experiencing and feeling at the moment.

Steps to Discipleship. *Call:* Jesus calls us to come and follow him in the way of life that he mapped out for us. He asks us to imitate him as we meet the events of every day living. As we listen we shall become more aware of his daily invitation to be like him.

Conditioning: As disciples we must be willing to give up our own ambitions and desires in order to concentrate on what the Lord is asking of us. There will be times of testing in order to strengthen our resolve and it may not be easy. Jesus made this quite clear: "If anyone wishes to come after me, he must deny himself and take up his cross daily and follow me" (Lk 9:23).

Commitment: When we recognize the Lord's calling, we must be prepared to say our yes to that invitation. This kind of commitment requires faith on our part. Mary's commitment is an ideal example. After she was enlightened about how the Lord's will was to take place within her, she gave her unconditional *fiat* in those memorable words: "May it be done to me according to your word" (Lk 1:38).

Qualifications. We may be concerned about the qualifications required to become a true disciple of the Lord. To remove any doubt or fear, we look to the first disciples themselves. The apostles were uneducated, uncouth, and of humble origin, yet they were gently called and led by Jesus. He even gave them a dignity above that of the patriarchs of the Old Testament times. God's gifts and graces equipped them for the vocation to which they were called. The same generous, gracious Lord is eager to make us equally competent to fulfill his mission for us. Daily prayer with Scripture will prepare us for discipleship, as St. Paul assures us: "All scripture is inspired by God and is useful for teaching, for refutation, for correction, and for training in righteousness, so that one who belongs to God may be competent, equipped for every good work" (2 Tm 3:16-17).

The calling of the first disciples should move us to a great spirit of gratitude. We are grateful that God saw fit to establish his kingdom on earth, that these disciples generously responded to that call, that disciples of Jesus continued through the centuries to pass down to us the faith and, finally, that God has also called us to be his disciples.

Scriptural Passage for Prayer

Be with Jesus on the day after his baptism as he encounters his first would-be disciples. Stay close to Jesus and listen with all your heart:

The next day John was there again with two of his disciples, and as he watched Jesus walk by, he said, "Behold, the Lamb of

God." The two disciples heard what he said and followed Jesus. Jesus turned and saw them following him and said to them, "What are you looking for?" They said to him, "Rabbi" (which translated means Teacher), "where are you staying?" He said to them, "Come, and you will see." So they went and saw where he was staying, and they stayed with him that day. It was about four in the afternoon. Andrew, the brother of Simon Peter, was one of the two who heard John and followed Jesus. He first found his own brother Simon and told him, "We have found the Messiah" (which is translated Anointed). Then he brought him to Jesus. Jesus looked at him and said, "You are Simon the son of John; you will be called Kephas" (which is translated Peter). The next day he decided to go to Galilee, and he found Philip. And Jesus said to him, "Follow me." Now Philip was from Bethsaida, the town of Andrew and Peter. Philip found Nathanael and told him, "We have found the one about whom Moses wrote in the law, and also the prophets, Jesus son of Joseph, from Nazareth." But Nathanael said to him, "Can anything good come from Nazareth?" Philip said to him, "Come and see." Jesus saw Nathanael coming toward him and said of him, "Here is a true Israelite. There is no duplicity in him." Nathanael said to him, "How do you know me?" Jesus answered and said to him, "Before Philip called you, I saw you under the fig tree." Nathanael answered him, "Rabbi, you are the Son of God; you are the King of Israel." Jesus answered and said to him, "Do you believe because I told you that I saw you under the fig tree? You will see greater things than this." And he said to him, "Amen, amen, I say to you, you will see the sky opened and the angels of God ascending and descending on the Son of Man." Jn. 1:35-51

Reflections

The following are a few thoughts which you can use in entering into prayer and contemplation.

... *"Behold the Lamb of God."* (v. 36)
In these words John proclaimed Jesus as the Messiah. He is the King who is calling us into his service.

... "Come, and you will see." ... (v. 39)

This was not an invitation to see the place where Jesus was dwelling, probably a pilgrim hut along the Jordan. Rather, it is an invitation to come and see who Jesus is, to hear his teaching, and also to come and pray with him.

... "Can anything good come from Nazareth?" ... (v. 46)

Nazareth was a backward village in Galilee. It was a common opinion that no prophet would ever come from Nazareth. God's ways are not our ways. Jesus came in poverty and humility and he began his ministry in the same style.

"... I saw you under the fig tree." (v. 48)

There is a deeper implication here. Perhaps Nathanael was having some kind of experience which no one could know about. Jesus' comment was significant enough to elicit an act of faith from Nathanael: "You are the King of Israel."

Moving Out of Prayer

Thank the Lord for the love, trust, and confidence he had in you when he called you to his way of life. You may wish to record specific incidents in your life when his clarion call was unmistakably clear.

Texts for Additional Days of Prayer

When Jesus called his followers, they did not immediately leave family and friends to work full-time at their apostolate. There were three stages to this call and final commitment. The following scriptural texts will help us to appreciate more the nature of our own call and help us to be better prepared to make our own commitment.

John 1:35-51: *First Call*—"... Come and you will see...." (v. 39) (already considered)

Luke 5:1-11:	*Second Call*—..."Do not be afraid; from now on you will be catching men." (v. 10)
Mark 3:13-15:	*Third Call*—"He appointed twelve [whom he also called apostles] that they might be with him..." (v. 14)
Luke 9:23-26:	..."If anyone wishes to come after me,..." (v. 23)
Luke 9:57-62:	..."I will follow you..." (v. 57)
Philippians 3:7-16:	"Whatever gains I had, these I have come to consider a loss because of Christ." (v. 7)

TWELVE

Jesus Teaches Us the Way

...*"Good Teacher, what must I do to inherit eternal life?"* **Mk 10:17**

Orientation

Jesus came into the world as a teacher. He is the Word of the Father, the revelation of the Father. Jesus came to teach us the good news of God's unconditional love for us and his ardent desire to have us be happy with him for all eternity. Jesus came to show us the way.

Jesus is an acknowledged teacher. Others called him rabbi, master, and teacher. Even his enemies addressed him this way. His disciples often used the title *rabboni*, a term of endearment, meaning "my teacher."

We can teach in various ways. We can use an intellectual method to present a mathematical proposition. Or we can use experimentation and observation. In teaching psychologically, we endeavor to have the person recognize his or her own problem and resolve to take steps to overcome it. However, the only way we can teach a spiritual truth is by witnessing to it in our own lives. We must live what we teach spiritually.

Jesus' teaching not only imparted information and truth, but he lived the way of life he was proposing for his followers. His teaching and his lifestyle reveal his personality and show the nature of the Father. Jesus lived what he preached.

Always and Everywhere. Jesus taught on every possible occasion. He could explain a profound theological truth in simple ordinary language so his hearers could comprehend it. He could shed light on the great mysteries of God by using concrete parables and figures of speech which we as well as his audiences can understand.

Any time a crowd gathered around him, Jesus was eager to instruct them about the reign of God. He often took the disciples off to a quiet place so that he could instruct them privately. He taught as he journeyed from one place to another. He also taught privately as he did when Nicodemus came to him at night.

Above all Jesus' whole life gave witness to what he was teaching. He did not merely say: "Love your enemies, and pray for those who persecute you" (Mt 5:44), but he reached out in loving concern, even to those who considered him an enemy. At his death he not only prayed for his enemies, he excused them: "Father, forgive them, they know not what they do" (Lk 23:34).

As a teacher, Jesus did not only advocate a life of poverty and detachment from the things of this world, but he could say of himself: "The Son of Man has nowhere to rest his head" (Lk 9:58).

Jesus did not merely teach us how to pray and encourage us to pray often, but gave us an example by his own life of prayer. Jesus prayed liturgically with his people: "He ... went according to his custom into the synagogue on the sabbath day" (Lk 4:16). He spent time in quiet prayer during his busy ministry: "Rising very early before dawn, he left and went off to a deserted place, where he prayed" (Mk 1:35). Jesus often prayed on location as he ministered to the people: "Then Jesus took the loaves, gave thanks, and distributed them to those who were reclining..." (Jn 6:11).

Self-Image. Since we are not only to follow his instructions, but also to imitate Jesus' way of living, we may often wonder what Jesus was really like. We have no picture or portrait to show us what Jesus was like physically. We do not even have a verbal description. Was he tall or short, thin or stocky, light or dark complexioned? The Scriptures tell us nothing about his physical appearance, but they do give us a wonderful composite portrait of his personality.

Jesus succinctly summarized his way of life and his own personality when he taught us the beatitudes. They are the *Magna Carta* of Christianity, the essence of how we are to live. They might be called the wisdom literature of the New Testament in a nutshell. In the beatitudes, Jesus was telling us that he is poor in spirit, merciful, single-hearted, and a bearer of genuine peace.

In our prayer we will receive some profound insights. We will remember that Jesus asks us to become his disciples. A disciple should be recognizable as a follower of Jesus, and have the same mind, heart, and attitude as the Master. In order to become a true disciple, we must know Jesus intimately and personally.

In the beatitudes, Jesus reveals his personality, and invites us to imitate him. In effect Jesus is saying: "I am poor in spirit and if you wish to be my disciple, then you, too, must be poor in spirit, and then you will be blessed." Make Jesus' revelation of self and encouragement to imitate him the basis of your prayer today.

Scriptural Passage for Prayer

Before you select one of the beatitudes on which to center your prayer, read all of them as a composite picture of the way of life recommended by Jesus. Under the guidance of the Holy Spirit, you may decide to pray over one beatitude for each of the next eight days. Or if you only have one day, select a beatitude that seems to speak most directly to your particular situation. Listen to the words of Jesus:

"Blessed are the poor in spirit,
   for theirs is the kingdom of heaven.
Blessed are they who mourn,
   for they will be comforted.
Blessed are the meek,
   for they will inherit the land.
Blessed are they who hunger and thirst for righteousness,
   for they will be satisfied.

Blessed are the merciful,
   for they will be shown mercy.
Blessed are the clean of heart,
   for they will see God.
Blessed are the peacemakers,
   for they will be called children of God.
Blessed are they who are persecuted for the sake of
      righteousness,
   for theirs is the kingdom of heaven.
Blessed are you when they insult you and persecute you and utter every kind of evil against you [falsely] because of me. Rejoice and be glad, for your reward will be great in heaven. Thus they persecuted the prophets who were before you."

Mt 5:3-12

Reflections

Of the many Scriptures which confirm Jesus' lifestyle to be in conformity with the beatitudes we have selected only one for each beatitude. You may choose others on your own.

"Blessed are the poor in spirit, ..." (v. 3)
"Foxes have dens and birds of the sky have nests, but the Son of Man has nowhere to rest his head." (Lk 9:58)

"Blessed are they who mourn, ..." (v. 4)
"As he drew near, he saw the city and wept over it." (Lk 19:41)

"Blessed are the meek, ..." (v. 5)
"Can anything good come from Nazareth?"(Jn 1:46)

"Blessed are they who hunger and thirst for righteousness, ..." (v. 6)
"We have come to believe and are convinced that you are the Holy One of God." (Jn 6:69)

"Blessed are the merciful, ..." (v. 7)
"Father, forgive them, they know not what they do, ..." (Lk 23:34)

"Blessed are the clean of heart, ..." (v. 8)
"Can any of you charge me with sin? ..." (Jn 8:46)

"Blessed are the peacemakers, . . ." (v. 9)
"Peace I leave with you; my peace I give to you. . . ." (Jn 14:27)

"Blessed are they who are persecuted . . ." (v. 10)
". . . If they persecuted me, they will also persecute you. . . ." (Jn 15:20)

Moving Out of Prayer

Move out of your prayer posture by praying the Lord's Prayer as found in Matthew 6:9-15. In your journal tell Jesus which personality trait impressed you most and how you hope to emulate it in your own life.

Texts for Additional Days of Prayer

For a summary of some of the teaching of Jesus, read reflectively the whole Sermon on the Mount: Matthew chapters 5, 6, and 7.

Jesus gives some additional insights into prayer in:

Matthew 6:5-15:	"But when you pray, go to your inner room, close the door, and pray to your Father in secret. . . ." (v. 6)
Matthew 7:7-11:	"Ask and it will be given to you; . . ." (v. 7)

THIRTEEN

Jesus the Healer

... "Master, I want to see." ...
"Go your way; your faith has saved
you." ... **Mk 10:51-52**

Orientation

If we want to know Jesus with a deep, appreciative heart knowledge, we must look to what he tells us about himself, or what he reveals about himself by his actions and attitudes. We can learn a great deal about Jesus from other sources, but we can know him as a person only by his self-revelation in the Scriptures.

Jesus came into our world to be our Savior and Healer. From the outset of his public ministry, he manifested his boundless love by healing every ailing person who really wanted to be healed. His healings were wholistic: he always healed the whole person physically, psychologically, and spiritually.

Jesus healed in every conceivable area. The Gospel is full of accounts of his many and varied healings. Jesus' healings did manifest his divine power, but that was not his primary reason for healing. He healed because he loved. He longed to heal all who were in pain or suffering in any way.

Jesus wanted to be known as a healer. When John the Baptist was arrested and put in prison, he sent some of his disciples to Jesus to ask him: "Are you the one who is to come or should we look for another?" (Mt 11:3).

Jesus answered their question—not by pointing to the fact that he was fulfilling the prophecies (as he did on the road to Emmaus)—by pointing to his healing ministry. "Go and tell John what you hear and see: the blind regain their sight, the lame walk, lepers are cleansed, the deaf hear, the dead are raised, and the poor have the good news proclaimed to them" (Mt 11:4-5).

Jesus' healings infuriated his enemies. They could not deny them: they were too evident. So they ascribed them to the action of Satan: "This man drives out demons only by the power of Beelzebul, the prince of demons" (Mt 12:24).

Jesus is now in his glory, but his glory consists in continuing his healing mission in the world today. "Jesus Christ is the same yesterday, today, and forever" (Heb 13:8).

Jesus healed many lepers. In his time, leprosy was a loathsome disease. A leper had to live in total isolation, exiled from family and friends, and banished from society. The prescriptions of the law were very strict (Leviticus 13 and 14, especially 13:45-46), and lepers were shunned and despised by everyone. It was commonly believed that lepers were guilty of some grave wrongdoing, for which God was punishing them. The lepers soon began to hate themselves. The psychological consequences were as serious as the physical. The fact that leprosy was terminal increased their sufferings.

Scriptural Passage for Prayer

Be with Jesus as he heals the leper who came to him with the desperate plea: "Lord, if you wish, you can make me clean."

Now there was a man full of leprosy in one of the towns where he was; and when he saw Jesus, he fell prostrate, pleaded with him, and said, "Lord, if you wish, you can make me clean." Jesus stretched out his hand, touched him, and said, "I do will it. Be made clean." And the leprosy left him immediately. Then he ordered him not to tell anyone, but "Go, show yourself to the priest and offer for your cleansing what Moses prescribed; that will be proof for them." The report about him spread all the more, and great crowds assembled to listen to him and to be cured of their ailments, but he would withdraw to deserted places to pray. **Lk 5:12-16**

Reflections

In this Gospel account, the leper left his isolation at great risk. He could have been stoned by anyone he met. He must have hidden behind anything which could conceal him until he saw his one chance. He dashed out to Jesus with an agonizing plea: "If you will do so, you can cure me." How heartrending his plea! How it must have touched the heart of Jesus.

As you contemplate this Gospel episode, look beyond the scene, the happenings, the persons involved. Look into the heart of Jesus. Try to experience what he must have experienced.

Permit the scene to be a sort of window through which you can behold divinity. Let it become a doorway through which you enter into the very presence of the Lord.

Rest and bask in that presence. Listen to all the nuances of what is happening. Linger with Jesus. Listen with your heart.

Jesus stretched out his hand, touched him, . . . (v. 13)
Jesus touched the man in order to comfort him. He let the leper know that even though society rejected him, he accepted him.

. . . "I do will it. Be made clean." . . . (v. 13)
The instant response of his loving heart to a desperate soul crying out to him was one of compassion. Jesus is revealing very much about himself. Jesus set the tone for the members of his kingdom. A true follower of Jesus, a dedicated disciple must touch the untouchable, love the unlovable, forgive the unforgivable.

. . . "Go, show yourself to the priest" . . . (v. 14)
Israel was a theocracy. The priests were civil rulers as well as religious. They had the right to determine whether a person was sufficiently healed to be readmitted to society. Jesus had another motive in mind. He wanted the priests to recognize his divine healing power, hoping that it would enkindle a spark of faith within them.

. . . but he would withdraw to deserted places to pray. (v. 16)
Jesus did not want the crowds to come to him simply to receive a healing. He wanted them to come because they believed in him. Jesus was a man of prayer. He probably wanted to thank the Father for this healing just accomplished and the encouragement it brought to the crowds to listen to him.
Jesus touched the untouchable.

Moving Out of Prayer

You may wish to write a "thank-you" note to Jesus for the many times he has healed you.

Texts for Additional Days of Prayer

If you wish to develop further your contemplation of Jesus as the Healer, the following passages may be helpful. They represent various ways in which Jesus healed.

Mark 10:46-52:	Blind Bartimaeus
Luke 7:11-17:	Raising to life of the son of the widow of Nain.
Luke 7:36-50:	Healing the sinfulness of the penitent woman.
Mark 2:1-12:	Healing the paralytic
Luke 9:37-43:	Healing the possessed boy

FOURTEEN

Who Is Jesus for Me?

> ... "Who do people say that
> the Son of Man is? ..."
> "But who do you say that I am?"
> **Mt 16:13-15**

Orientation

At Caesarea Philippi we hear Jesus asking the apostles and us: "Who do you say that I am?" (Mt 16:15). This is a question we must ask ourselves every day. Who is Jesus for me?

Each day Jesus reveals himself in a new and different way. As we get to know him more intimately and personally, we can really begin to love him.

As Jesus was about to start his mission of redemptive suffering, he chose to make an extraordinary revelation about himself. Jesus went up to Mt. Tabor to let the three apostles in his inner circle witness his divinity.

Mt. Tabor is a sugarloaf mountain rising up alone in the plain of Esdralen. Its summit is 1,500 feet above the valley floor. It forms a perfect altar under the azure blue cathedral-like vault of heaven. With Mt. Tabor's view of the fertile valley below, Mt. Hermon on the north, and Mt. Gerazim on the south, it is one of the most picturesque spots in Israel. Jesus chose to bring his inner circle of three apostles here to spend time in prayer and to let them experience a deeper insight into his personality and mission.

Developing Faith. The apostles did not immediately recognize Jesus as the God-Man. Their faith grew gradually. At first they acknowledged Jesus as a rabbi and teacher, then they recognized him as a prophet. Gradually their faith developed so they could identify him as the prophet and divine messenger foretold by Malachi (3:1).

At Caesarea Philippi, Peter's profession of faith was not quite a total recognition of Jesus as God, but certainly a very important messenger sent by God. Only after the coming of the Holy Spirit did they recognize his divinity. The early Christian community as a whole professed their faith in Jesus as God. The transfiguration was a gigantic step forward in their developing faith.

Why the Transfiguration? The time of his death was rapidly approaching. Jesus knew that all would be scandalized by his fate. Their hopes and expectations would be crushed since their vision of the Messiah was so diametrically different than the truth he was revealing.

For this reason Jesus took his "prayer team," Peter, James, and John, to the summit of Mt. Tabor so that they could witness for a brief moment the splendor of his divinity radiating through his humanity. The experience was so overwhelming that "they fell silent and did not at that time tell anyone what they had seen" (Lk 9:36). This other-worldly vision strengthened the faith of the apostles so that they could be pillars of faith to confirm the faith of others.

It appears that Jesus went up on the mountain to pray in order to know the Father's will more clearly for his mission. In prayer he was able to accept the dreadful mission which lay ahead. Only after his yes to the Father was he transfigured.

The Father does the same for us. When we come to him in prayer he reveals himself, his loving concern, his awareness of the problems which face us, and his eagerness to strengthen our faith.

The appearance of Moses, the lawgiver, and Elijah, the prophet, attested to the authenticity of the redemptive passion and death of Jesus. At the river Jordan when Jesus was baptized and prepared to begin his teaching mission, the Father confirmed the ministry of Jesus. "This is my beloved Son, with whom I am well pleased" (Mt

3:17). Now the Father confirmed his mission of suffering and death: "This is my chosen Son; listen to him" (Lk 9:35).

St. Leo the Great offers some valuable insights into the fruits of the Transfiguration:

> The great reason for this transfiguration was to remove the scandal of the cross from the hearts of the disciples, and to prevent the humiliation of his voluntary suffering from disturbing the faith of those who had witnessed the surpassing glory that lay concealed.
>
> With no less forethought he was also providing a firm foundation for the whole Church. The whole body of Christ was to understand the kind of transformation that it would receive as a gift. The members of that body were to look forward to a share in that glory which first blazed out in Christ their head. (*Liturgy of Hours*, Vol. II, Second Sunday of Lent, p. 149)

As we rest quietly and prayerfully with Jesus on Mt. Tabor, we, too, can say humbly and sincerely with St. Peter: "Master, it is good that we are here."

Scriptural Passage for Prayer

As you listen to the Gospel version of the Transfiguration, pray for the grace that you, too, might witness the splendor of the Lord. Luke relates this unique event in these words:

> About eight days after he said this, he took Peter, John, and James and went up the mountain to pray. While he was praying his face changed in appearance and his clothing became dazzling white. And behold, two men were conversing with him, Moses and Elijah, who appeared in glory and spoke of his exodus that he was going to accomplish in Jerusalem. Peter and his companions had been overcome by sleep, but becoming fully awake, they saw his glory and the two men standing with him. As they were about to part from him, Peter said to Jesus, "Master, it is good that we are here; let us make three tents, one

for you, one for Moses, and one for Elijah." But he did not know what he was saying. While he was still speaking, a cloud came and cast a shadow over them, and they became frightened when they entered the cloud. Then from the cloud came a voice that said, "This is my chosen Son; listen to him." After the voice had spoken, Jesus was found alone. They fell silent and did not at that time tell anyone what they had seen. **Lk 9:28-30**

Reflections

Throughout the Gospel Jesus continues to reveal more and more about himself by everything he says and does. Metaphorically he makes some direct statements about himself which are commonly called the "I am" passages. As you contemplate these statements you will come to know Jesus as a loving, caring, concerned, personal God whose unconditional love is poured out on anyone who will receive it. Listen with your heart as Jesus says:

... *"I am the light of the world. Whoever follows me will not walk in darkness, but will have the light of life."* (Jn 8:12)
Light in the scriptural language always symbolizes the presence of God. Jesus calls himself the light of life. Flowers cannot bloom without the light of the sun. The abiding presence of Jesus with his grace and life in our life will lead us to eternal life.

... *"I am the way and the truth and the life. . . ."* (Jn 14:6)
Jesus came to teach us a way of life which would bring us peace, joy, and happiness in this life and lead us to our eternal union with him. He not only taught us the way, but he lived it himself as a model and example for us.

". . . I am the good shepherd, and I know mine and mine know me, . . ." (Jn 10:14)
The figure of the sheep and the shepherd, portraying God as shepherd and his people as the flock, is used frequently throughout Scripture. A shepherd loves his sheep. He feeds and protects them. Jesus calls himself the Good Shepherd to assure us of his caring, concerned love for us.

". . . I am the vine, you are the branches. . . ." (Jn 15:5)
The indwelling of the Godhead within us is certainly a great

mystery which baffles our understanding. Jesus explains this sublime truth with a simple allegory. Since contemplation gives us insights beyond analysis try to plumb more deeply this comforting truth.

... *"I am the bread of life; whoever comes to me will never hunger, and whoever believes in me will never thirst. ..."* (Jn 6:35)
Jesus prepares us for the gift of himself in the Eucharist. If we accept this truth with a lively, committed faith, Jesus promises that he will never reject us, but will raise us up on the last day. Respond in praise and thanksgiving for this heavenly gift.

... *"I am the resurrection and the life; whoever believes in me, even if he dies, will live, and everyone who lives and believes in me will never die. ..."* (Jn 11:25-26)
How often Jesus promised eternal life to those who believe in him! Our faith must be a dynamic, operative faith which enables us to live the way of life Jesus mapped out for us.

Jesus rose from the dead so that he could share his glorified life with us in part here in this land of exile and in all his fullness at the moment of our death. Do we need further proof of his infinite love?

Moving Out of Prayer

Slowly and repeatedly make a simple act of faith, such as: "I do believe, Lord. Help my lack of faith."
In your journal tell Jesus who and what he means to you.

Texts for Additional Days of Prayer

Matthew 17:1-8:	Story of Transfiguration
Peter 1:17-19:	"... while we were with him on the holy mountain." (v. 18)

In the Old Testament there are many theophanies by means of which the Lord manifests not only his presence, but also his glory, power, and loving concern. This occurs frequently throughout the Psalms. Here are a few examples offered for your prayer time:

Exodus 13:21-22:	"The LORD preceded them, in the daytime by means of a column of cloud to show them the way, and at night by means of a column of fire to give them light...." (v. 21)
Exodus 19:16-19:	"Mount Sinai was all wrapped in smoke, for the LORD came down upon it in fire...." (v. 18)
1 Kings 19:11-13:	"... After the fire there was a tiny whispering sound." (v. 12)
Psalm 19:2-7:	"The heavens declare the glory of God, ..." (v. 2)
Psalm 29:1-11:	"... the voice of the Lord is majestic." (v. 4)

FIFTEEN

Jesus Raises Lazarus to Life

For if we have grown into union with him through a death like his, we shall also be united with him in the resurrection. **Rom 6:5**

Introduction

St. John recorded this story of Jesus restoring life to Lazarus at great length; hence it is divided into three separate units, one for each period of prayer. You may choose to focus on one in listening prayer or use all three. In any case, it would be advantageous to read the whole episode reflectively and permit the Holy Spirit to lead you.

Orientation

The raising of Lazarus to life portends the fate of Jesus. It was as if he were signing his own death warrant. The antagonism of his enemies was rapidly increasing. They were desperate since they could neither discredit him nor prevent him from teaching and healing. Their hatred did not daunt Jesus. He fearlessly continued to proclaim the good news of the kingdom as the Father wished.

In this episode Jesus revealed more about himself as a person. He manifested his loving concern for his friends and the deep personal feelings which filled his heart. By raising Lazarus from the dead, Jesus proved his power of life and death which added great credibility to everything he was teaching. He was thrilled to bring joy and consolation to Martha and Mary and to all of us by promising that we would rise to enjoy the eternal bliss of heaven.

Prayer Period One

Scriptural Passage for Prayer.

> Now a man was ill, Lazarus from Bethany, the village of Mary and her sister Martha. Mary was the one who had anointed the Lord with perfumed oil and dried his feet with her hair; it was her brother Lazarus who was ill. So the sisters sent word to him, saying, "Master, the one you love is ill." When Jesus heard this he said, "This illness is not to end in death, but is for the glory of God, that the Son of God may be glorified through it." Now Jesus loved Martha and her sister and Lazarus. Jn 11:1-5

Reflections. This is a lengthy passage (44 verses) and since our moods vary from time to time, no specific or detailed reflections are offered here. Ask the Holy Spirit to guide you to that word or expression which will launch you into a contemplative prayer posture. You may be inclined to spend time comforting Martha or Mary, or to tell Jesus how much you appreciate his humanness in becoming "perturbed and deeply troubled," or you may wish to linger with Jesus as he wept, or even to help to "untie him (Lazarus) and let him go."

Prayer Period Two

Scriptural Passage for Prayer.

> When Jesus arrived, . . . Martha said to Jesus, "Lord, if you had been here, my brother would not have died. [But] even now I know that whatever you ask of God, God will give you." Jesus said to her, "Your brother will rise." Martha said to him, "I know he will rise, in the resurrection on the last day." Jesus told her, "I

am the resurrection and the life; whoever believes in me, even if he dies, will live, and everyone who lives and believes in me will never die. Do you believe this?" She said to him, "Yes, Lord. I have come to believe that you are the Messiah, the Son of God, the one who is coming into the world." Jn 11:17-27

Reflections. In these verses, the word "believe" is used four times; three times by Jesus and once by Martha. Jesus always asks for an abiding faith in him, and is pleased when he finds this faith. Likewise, he is disappointed when he discovers a lack of faith. In Nazareth he could not work any miracles of healing because of their lack of faith.

Martha expressed faith in the resurrection to come. She did not have any clear idea of what the resurrection entailed at this time, but she knew that Jesus had promised eternal life on many occasions.

Jesus took the occasion to enlighten her and us further about our own personal resurrection. Jesus explained that he is the resurrection and the life. His redemption makes it possible for us to share in his risen glorified life, at least partially in this life and fully after our death.

Yes, we must die to this physical existence so that we can rise as Jesus did to a new and fuller life in glory. Martha's final act of faith is total. She believes that Jesus is "the Messiah, the Son of God." With this conviction there is no cause for anxiety, for everything will transpire as God wills.

Such a profession of faith encourages us all the more to pray in the words of the father of the possessed boy: "I do believe, help my unbelief!" (Mk 9:24).

Prayer Period Three

Scriptural Passage for Prayer.

When Mary came to where Jesus was and saw him, she fell at his feet and said to him, "Lord, if you had been here, my brother would not have died." When Jesus saw her weeping and the Jews who had come with her weeping, he became perturbed and deeply troubled, and said, "Where have you laid him?"

They said to him, "Sir, come and see." And Jesus wept. So the Jews said, "See how he loved him." But some of them said, "Could not the one who opened the eyes of the blind man have done something so that this man would not have died?"

So Jesus, perturbed again, came to the tomb. It was a cave, and a stone lay across it. Jesus said, "Take away the stone." Martha, the dead man's sister, said to him, "Lord, by now there will be a stench; he has been dead for four days." Jesus said to her, "Did I not tell you that if you believe you will see the glory of God?" So they took away the stone. And Jesus raised his eyes and said, "Father, I thank you for hearing me. I know that you always hear me; but because of the crowd here I have said this, that they may believe that you sent me." And when he had said this, he cried out in a loud voice, "Lazarus, come out!" The dead man came out, tied hand and foot with burial bands, and his face was wrapped in a cloth. So Jesus said to them, "Untie him and let him go." Jn 11:32-44

Reflections. In his human nature Jesus experienced all the emotions which we feel. He knew sorrow and pain, joy and happiness. At the tomb of Lazarus, Jesus experienced the same pain of separation felt by Mary and Martha, and it caused him to weep. He, too, felt the loss of a friend.

Jesus always prayed on location before or after many of the incidents in his life. Here we hear him turning to the Father and praying: "Father, I thank you for hearing me. . . ." Jesus' frequent and constant prayer is a compelling example for us.

As we listen to Jesus crying out with a loud voice: "Lazarus come out!" we can feel the tension in this moment pregnant with anticipation and expectancy. The quiet of that moment must have been shattered by the reaction of the crowd as Lazarus emerged "tied hand and foot with burial bands." When the Lord makes his power and his presence felt in any given situation, there is always an air of awe and reverence. We respond by raising our hearts in praise and thanksgiving.

The brief command of Jesus, "untie him and let him go," has a twofold meaning. First, Jesus calls upon the community to help Lazarus. With his power over life and death Jesus certainly could have untied Lazarus himself by a mere act of his will. However,

Jesus wants to work through us the members of his body. We are called to a life of loving service to our neighbor.

Second, Jesus was reminding us that we can easily bind another person by our attitude toward him or her, by our constant criticism, by our lack of appreciation, by our refusal to love, by our lack of acceptance. In fact, any lack of love can bind another person.

From this scriptural event, we can learn once again how very much Jesus loved. He admonishes us: "As I have loved you, so you also should love one another" (Jn 13:34).

Moving Out of Prayer

Thank Jesus for his solemn promise of resurrection at the close of your life. In the journal tell Jesus what thrilled you most in this story.

Texts for Additional Days of Prayer

For continued prayer you will find a direct contrast between God's love and the hatred of the enemies of Jesus:

Luke 11:45-54:	"... for they were plotting to catch him at something he might say." (v. 54)
1 John 4:1-21:	"... for God is love." (v. 8)
Luke 7:11-17:	"... Young man, I tell you, arise!" (v. 14)
Luke 8:40-42, 49-56:	"But he took her by the hand and called to her, 'Child arise!' " (v.54)
Romans 6:1-11:	"... just as Christ was raised from the dead by the glory of the Father, we too might live in newness of life." (v. 4)

Part Three:

The Son Redeems Us

PART THREE

Introduction

AS WE BEGIN TO CONTEMPLATE the passion and death of Jesus, we are reaching into the very heart of the Gospel. This is the focal point of salvation. In our prayer we must make a significant change in our attitude and approach to Jesus. It will be necessary to reorient our personal relationship with him.

We listened with enlightened interest to Jesus throughout his public ministry. In prayer we responded in love for the sake of our own spiritual growth. Yet this is not yet perfect love.

Now we begin to love Jesus with the purer love of genuine friendship. We must dare to love him for himself regardless of the benefits which may or may not accrue to us. This is the summit of Christian maturity; not to think of ourselves, but of Jesus, not to be concerned about receiving love, but about giving love. This is the heart of friendship.

Sadness or Sorrow

Our approach to the sufferings of Jesus in prayer must be carefully directed. If we would try to experience every lash, blow, humiliation, and pain which Jesus endured, it would lead us into sadness, but not sorrow.

Sadness arises from a sense of guilt. Guilt will deter us from a wrongdoing only for a period of time. As the sense of guilt diminishes, we could fall back into the same sin. It is also true that if guilt persists it will lead to discouragement, disappointment with ourselves, and ultimately to depression.

On the other hand, love begets genuine sorrow. If we love a person, we will be moved to sorrow for having offended that person. Love is a more powerful deterrent to avoid any offense since we do not wish to hurt the person we love.

The better approach then is to bring ourselves to the realization that the risen, glorified Jesus is living with us and within us. Together with him we can prayerfully relive what he suffered. This will lead us to genuine sorrow which springs from love. Try this simple procedure:

(a) Sit with the risen Jesus and together look back over all the events of his cruel passion. Let him explain to you that he willingly accepted all his sufferings because he loves us so much that he wanted to redeem us that we might be united with him for all eternity in perfect love.

(b) Jesus would remind us that his sufferings were his glorification. In fact, Jesus always refers to his sufferings as his glorification. Jesus suffered not to assuage the Father's anger, but to offer the Father the most perfect act of love that could ever be made by a human being.

(c) Relive the experience with Jesus in order to love Jesus for himself, asking for the grace to respond with greater gratitude, more compassion, and a more intense love. Love proves its authenticity through action. Love must give itself to the person loved. Therefore, we must be united with Jesus.

Fruits

A prayerful reliving of the passion with Jesus will bear much fruit, especially these:

(a) Our prayer will enkindle a genuine spirit of gratitude. Gratitude is usually in proportion to the gift given or the service rendered. Jesus gave us everything: the promise of heaven by the shedding of his last drop of blood. It was a complete *kenosis* (emptying). As we pray our gratitude will greatly increase.

(b) The overwhelming compassion of Jesus will inspire greater compassion in our own hearts. When we begin to appreciate that Jesus was willing to do so much for us, we will be motivated to reach out in greater compassion to all our brothers and sisters throughout the world.

(c) Jesus' love for us is infinite and unconditional. He assured us of this himself: "No one has greater love than this, . . ." (Jn 15:13). The outpouring of his boundless love for us will inflame our hearts with a greater, more perfect love for him. It will not be a selfish love, but the love of true friendship. This kind of love will lead us into sorrow for our sinfulness instead of a sadness which only produces morbidity and guilt. Genuine sorrow has a more compelling power to help us avoid sin.

As we pray for the spirit of compassion, the Lord will endow us with a greater capacity to suffer along with him and other members of his body. St. Paul underscores the necessity of our personal participation with Jesus in his redemptive work. Notice the Greek preposition "syn," "with": "I suffer WITH Christ (Rom 8:17)—I am nailed to the cross WITH Christ (Col 2:4)—I die WITH Christ (2 Tim 2:11)—I am buried WITH Christ (Col 2:12)—I am raised from death WITH Christ (Rom 6:4)—I am carried into heaven WITH Christ (Rom 6:11) and am seated WITH Christ at the right hand of the Father" (Col 3:1).

Let us proceed by asking Jesus to accompany us as we try to relive his passion, death, and resurrection prayerfully, gratefully, lovingly, and compassionately.

SIXTEEN

Entry Into Jerusalem

"Hosanna to the Son of David;
blessed is he who comes in the name of the
Lord; hosanna in the highest." Mt 21:9

Orientation

After Jesus raised Lazarus to life, the people began to realize that Jesus was more than a great prophet. Here was a man with power over life and death itself. They were hoping that he was the Messiah who would free them from the domination of Rome. With his triumphal entry into the holy city, they expected him to announce his kingship and deliver Israel.

As this exuberant procession moved along, Jesus encountered three groups who held different attitudes toward him. The first group, his enemies, were motivated by hatred, envy and hostility. They tried to discredit him in the eyes of the people. As religious leaders of the people, they asked Jesus to stop the crowd from crying out in joy along the parade route, since they perceived him as a direct threat to their power.

The second group were the curious. They had heard of the miraculous raising of Lazarus and had come with the hope of witnessing some sensational event. Their curiosity made them intent on what was taking place, but their heart was far from the way of life which Jesus was teaching.

The third group were the believers. These were the followers of

Jesus whose faith in him was being enkindled more and more. These early disciples sang out enthusiastically: "Blessed is the King who comes in the name of the Lord."

Today's Attitudes. The reception Jesus receives in our day is very much the same. Jesus has his enemies in our times: professed atheists and self-proclaimed agnostics; and then hosts of people who are somewhat curious but largely indifferent to him. Like the people in his own times, Jesus is not the type of Messiah they want. His whole way of life is a condemnation of the way they want to live.

Also today there are those who expect the Lord to do something for them. They may come to him in their need to beg for an instant remedy for a problem—be it restoration to good health or a solution to some major personal difficulty. They want the Lord to be a bountiful Father to them when they cry out to him, but seldom have time for him otherwise.

Happily, the dedicated and devoted disciples of Jesus who love him dearly are also still here. They want to sing his praises and declare the good news to everyone they meet. As disciples, they not only accompany Jesus on his triumphal entry into Jerusalem, they also walk on his way of the cross. Come what may they joyously sing their hosannas.

Scriptural Passage for Prayer

Listen intently and with an open heart to the account as presented by Matthew 21:1-11.

When they drew near Jerusalem and came to Bethphage on the Mount of Olives, Jesus sent two disciples, saying to them, "Go into the village opposite you, and immediately you will find an ass tethered, and a colt with her. Untie them and bring them here to me. And if anyone should say anything to you, reply, 'The Master has need of them.' Then he will send them at once." This happened so that what had been spoken through the prophet might be fulfilled:
"Say to daughter Zion,

'Behold, your king comes to you,
meek and riding on an ass,
and on a colt, the foal of a beast of burden.' "

The disciples went and did as Jesus had ordered them. They brought the ass and the colt and laid their cloaks over them, and he sat upon them. The very large crowd spread their cloaks on the road, while others cut branches from the trees and strewed them on the road. The crowds preceding him and those following kept crying out and saying:

"Hosanna to the Son of David;
blessed is he who comes in the name of the Lord;
hosanna in the highest."

And when he entered Jerusalem the whole city was shaken and asked, "Who is this?" And the crowds replied, "This is Jesus the prophet, from Nazareth in Galilee."

Reflections

A key expression in this scriptural account may stimulate your prayer as you visit with Jesus and the disciples on their procession into the holy city.

They brought the ass and the colt. . . . (v. 7)
Jesus had many friends who were willing to assist him at any time. Surely, the owner of the donkey must have been one of his friends; otherwise, it is doubtful that he would have given it up so readily. Jesus came into the world as the "Prince of Peace." The donkey is a symbol of peace, while the horse is used for war. Solomon, for example, rode a donkey to his coronation because he desired and prayed for a peaceful reign (1 Kgs 1:44).

. . . "Hosanna to the Son of David; . . ." (v. 9)
According to the accepted opinion of St. Jerome, Hosanna is a contraction of two words meaning "save me" or "save, we pray." This, too, can be a profession of faith in Jesus as the Messiah.

As he drew near, he saw the city and wept over it, saying, "If this day you only knew what makes for peace—but now it is hidden from your eyes."

Luke adds this detail to his account of the triumphal entry (19:41-42). Since his own people would not accept him nor believe in him, Jesus wept and lamented over their lack of faith in him. He had come to redeem them and give them the peace which the world cannot give—the peace and joy of the eternal happiness of heaven. But many would not accept him. Jesus also foresaw the destruction of the holy city at the hands of the Romans some few years later.

When they reached the temple area, Jesus withdrew to Mt. Olivet because he feared that the people would try to make him an earthly king. They did not yet fully understand that through his redemptive death and resurrection, he would establish a spiritual kingdom, not a temporal rule.

Moving Out of Prayer

Experience this bittersweet moment in Jesus' life. Pray that Jesus' tragic lament will become less frequent in our times. In your journal let your heart rejoice as you join the friends of Jesus singing:

"Hosanna to the Son of David;
blessed is he who comes in the name of the Lord; . . ."

Texts for Additional Days of Prayer

Each morning after his triumphal entry into Jerusalem, Jesus would return to continue his teaching and instruction to his followers. His enemies took the occasion to try to trap Jesus in his words so that they might discredit him. These teachings and events are conducive to further prayer.

Zechariah 9:9-10:	". . . See, your king shall come to you; . . ."
Matthew 21:12-17:	"My house shall be a house of prayer; . . ." (v. 13)

Matthew 22:34-41:	"You shall love the Lord, your God, with all your heart, . . ." (v. 37)
Matthew 22:1-14:	"The kingdom of heaven may be likened to a king who gave a wedding feast for his son. . . ." (v. 2)
Matthew 22:15-22:	"Then repay to Caesar what belongs to Caesar . . ." (v. 21)

SEVENTEEN

Jesus Gives Himself to Us in the Eucharist

"I am the living bread that came down from heaven; whoever eats this bread will live forever; . . ." Jn 6:51

Introduction

This contemplation on the Holy Eucharist drawn from John's Gospel is presented in three stages—the promise, the reaction of the crowd and the disciples, and the institution of the sacrament. Each unit furnishes abundant inspiration for prayer. It would be more profitable to use only one unit for each prayer period. If you only have time for one prayer period, let the Spirit guide you to the one most pertinent to you.

The Promise

Orientation. When Jesus redeemed our human nature he merited for us the potential of receiving his glorified, risen life. He came to abide with us and within us. However, Jesus was well aware how worldly our thinking is and how difficult it is for us to grasp a purely spiritual concept.

For this reason, he gave us a sign and a symbol of his abiding presence when he gave us himself in the Holy Eucharist under the appearance of bread and wine. A whole year before he instituted the Holy Eucharist he prepared us for this sublime truth by promising to give us himself as the "bread of life."

Scriptural Passage for Prayer.

> ... "I am the bread of life; whoever comes to me will never hunger, and whoever believes in me will never thirst. But I told you that although you have seen [me], you do not believe. Everything that the Father gives me will come to me, and I will not reject anyone who comes to me, because I came down from heaven not to do my own will but the will of the one who sent me. And this is the will of the one who sent me, that I should not lose anything of what he gave me, but that I should raise it [on] the last day. For this is the will of my Father, that everyone who sees the Son and believes in him may have eternal life, and I shall raise him [on] the last day." **Jn 6:35-40**

Reflections.

"... bread of life; ..." (v. 35)

This is a scriptural expression which means that God will supply all our needs. Jesus himself said: "whoever comes to me will never hunger, and whoever believes in me will never thirst." Jesus was not referring only to our physical needs, but he fulfills all our needs.

"... I will not reject anyone who comes to me, ..." (v. 37)

This is a divine promise and it is trustworthy. It is the source of great assurance and comfort to us.

"... I shall raise him [on] the last day." (v. 40)

Jesus' eucharistic gift of himself is a tangible sign and symbol of his abiding presence with us here on earth. It is also a powerful means for conditioning us to live in his presence for all eternity.

The Reaction of the Crowd and the Disciples

Orientation. Those people who came to Jesus seeking only temporal benefits were disappointed in him and refused to accept the eucharistic gift of himself. He seemed to demand too much of them because they lacked faith in him.

Scriptural Passage for Prayer.

> As a result of this, many [of] his disciples returned to their former way of life and no longer accompanied him. Jesus then said to the Twelve, "Do you also want to leave?" Simon Peter answered him, "Master, to whom shall we go? You have the words of eternal life. We have come to believe and are convinced that you are the Holy One of God." Jesus answered them, "Did I not choose you twelve? Yet is not one of you a devil?" He was referring to Judas, son of Simon the Iscariot; it was he who would betray him, one of the Twelve. Jn 6:66-71

Reflections.

> *... no longer accompanied him.* (v. 66)
> Try to feel the disappointment in Jesus' heart. This was to be his crowning gift, yet the faith of many was not sufficient to accept the gracious gift of himself. Pray for those who follow the same path today as they leave him because of their lack of faith. Thank the Lord for your gift of faith as a comfort and consolation to him.
>
> *... "Master, to whom shall we go?"* ... (v. 68)
> St. Peter's profession of faith was music to the ears of Jesus. Peter must have been joined by a chorus of affirmations from the other disciples. With Peter and the other apostles let us say: "You are the Holy One of God."

The Institution of the Sacrament

Orientation. The great moment had arrived for Jesus and for us. He had come into the world not as a guest, but to stay with us. Even though he is dwelling with us and within us in his divine life, he knew that we would need a more tangible sign and symbol to strengthen our faith. Here is St. Luke's account of the institution of the Holy Eucharist. In spirit go to the Upper Room with Jesus and his apostles. Stay close to Jesus. Keep your gaze fixed on him and listen with your heart.

Scriptural Passage for Prayer.

> When the hour came, he took his place at table with the apostles. He said to them, "I have eagerly desired to eat this Passover with you before I suffer, for, I tell you, I shall not eat it [again] until there is fulfillment in the kingdom of God." Then he took a cup, gave thanks, and said, "Take this and share it among yourselves; for I tell you [that] from this time on I shall not drink of the fruit of the vine until the kingdom of God comes." Then he took the bread, said the blessing, broke it, and gave it to them, saying, "This is my body, which will be given for you; do this in memory of me." And likewise the cup after they had eaten, saying, "This cup is the new covenant in my blood, which will be shed for you." Lk 22:14-20

Reflections.

> ... *"I have eagerly desired to eat this Passover with you . . ."* (v. 15)

Love seeks a close union with the person loved. The boundless love of Jesus for each one of us is so great that he devised this sacramental way of remaining with us and within us as our spiritual food and drink. This giving of himself brought him much joy, as our giving to others brings joy and satisfaction in our lives.

> *". . . for, I tell you, I shall not eat it [again] until there is fulfillment in the kingdom of God."* (v. 16)

Apparently Jesus was referring to the fourth cup of wine which the father of the family drank to the coming Messiah during the Passover meal. It seems that this was Jesus' way of telling his apostles that he is the Messiah. Since the Messiah has arrived and is now about to complete his redemptive mission, there is no further need to drink this cup.

> *Then he took the bread, said the blessing, broke it, and gave it to them, . . .* (v. 19)

The four verbs *took, blessed, broke,* and *gave,* illustrate the procedure which Jesus followed at the Last Supper and in the multiplication of the loaves. Jesus continues to sanctify everything he gives us.

". . . do this in memory of me." (v. 19)
What did Jesus really mean when he gave us this command? It loses much of its meaning in translation. Surely Jesus meant for us to continue to offer the Eucharist, but he meant much more.

In offering the Mass, Jesus gave us a marvelous way of presenting ourselves and all that we do to God. He accepts our gift and sanctifies it by uniting it with the gift of himself. He then presents it to the Father in our name.

He was also telling us to do what he had done. From his first breath in Bethlehem to his last gasp on the cross, Jesus had given himself totally and completely to the Father. This is what he requested of us when he instituted this unique method of giving ourselves to the Father.

Third, Jesus was identifying himself with us in so personal a way that we share in his priestly role. We are a privileged, priestly people as St. Peter says: "You are 'a chosen race, a royal priesthood, a holy nation, a people of his own, so that you may announce the praises' of him who called you out of darkness into his wonderful light." (1 Pt 2:9)

Moving Out of Prayer

In the words of the Apostle Thomas, make repeated acts of faith slowly and quietly: "My Lord and my God!"

If the Spirit so moves you try to note in your journal what life would be like without the presence of Jesus in the Eucharist.

Texts for Additional Days of Prayer

Luke 22:7-13:	Peter and John prepared for the Passover.
1 Corinthians 11:17-34:	Paul tries to correct some abuses regarding the celebration of the

Eucharist. The greater wonder is Paul's account of the institution of the Eucharist which was revealed to him privately. It parallels the Gospel account even though it was written before the Gospel.

Exodus 16:4-15:	... "This is the bread which the LORD has given you to eat." (v. 15)
Psalm 78:23-25:	"He rained manna upon them for food and gave them heavenly bread."
Acts 2:42-47:	"They devoted themselves ... to the breaking of the bread and to the prayers." (v. 42)

EIGHTEEN

Jesus' Discourse at the Last Supper

"Whoever loves me will keep my word, and my Father will love him, and we will come to him and make our dwelling with him." **Jn 14:23**

Introduction

Since this last discourse of Jesus (John 13:31-38 and chapters 14, 15, 16, 17) is quite long, it would be profitable to read it reflectively in its entirety. As you read, note various sections to which you wish to return for prayer. Only three short sections are highlighted in this presentation.

Jesus Encourages His Disciples

Orientation. This lengthy discourse of Jesus at the Last Supper might be called the homily of the first Mass offered by the eternal High Priest himself. Jesus wanted to bring comfort, hope, and reassurance to the apostles and to all of us. In doing so, he reveals his loving concern for us.

The final moments of a loved one's life are extremely precious. In those closing moments we speak only of those things which are important. We can be certain that Jesus spoke only of those matters which were uppermost in his heart, and which would be important to us even today in saying farewell to those we love.

In the Upper Room, Jesus is surrounded by his beloved apostles. The hour is rapidly approaching when he will be taken away from them. He will soon suffer the painful disappointment of being denied by one of his own, betrayed by another, and deserted by all.

Jesus was well aware of the hatred and jealousy, the plotting, and intrigue which were closing in on him. He had already experienced rejection by the leaders of his own people. Now their rejection would explode, terminating in his own crucifixion.

In spite of all this Jesus towered far above this avalanche of hatred and bitterness. Even though the forces of evil were relentlessly moving in against him, he is not concerned about himself. He does not indulge in self-pity. On the contrary, he is concerned only about us. Listen intently to what Jesus is saying to encourage, comfort, and console us, but do not stop there. In your prayer try to fathom what went on in the heart of Jesus. Strive to experience his feelings and emotions, while he speaks to us.

Scriptural Passage for Prayer. Jesus knew that we would be beset with anxieties and worries, with doubts and fears, with disappointments and discouragement. How pleased he must have been when he could encourage and assure us in these words:

> "Do not let your hearts be troubled. You have faith in God; have faith also in me. In my Father's house there are many dwelling places. If there were not, would I have told you that I am going to prepare a place for you? And if I go and prepare a place for you, I will come back again and take you to myself, so that where I am you also may be." **Jn 14:1-3**

Reflections.

". . . You have faith in God; have faith also in me." (v. 1)
When we step out in faith, our trust and confidence in God will increase leaving little or no room for worry, doubt, or anxiety. Our faith pleases Jesus immensely. He is asking us to believe and trust in his words to us.

"... I am going to prepare a place for you?" (v. 2)
Jesus was about to begin his passion and death by which we would be redeemed, enabling us to be united with him for all eternity. This is the dwelling he is preparing.

"... I will come back again and take you to myself, ..." (v. 3)
By his resurrection from the dead, Jesus made it possible for us to rise from the dead so that we may also be with him in glory.

The Commandment to Love

Orientation. God created us to love and be loved. That we might love ourselves and our neighbor as the Lord intends, we must first know deep within ourselves that God loves us just as we are. Only then can we accept ourselves and others just as we are.

Scriptural Passage for Prayer. In this final discourse Jesus' words are convincing:

> "As the Father loves me, so I also love you. Remain in my love. If you keep my commandments, you will remain in my love, just as I have kept my Father's commandments and remain in his love.
>
> "I have told you this so that my joy might be in you and your joy might be complete. This is my commandment: love one another as I love you. No one has greater love than this, to lay down one's life for one's friends. You are my friends if you do what I command you." Jn 15:9-14

Reflections.

"As the Father loves me, ..." (v. 9)
The Father loves Jesus with an infinite love, a perfect love. Jesus assures us that his love for us is equally great.

"Remain in my love. ..." (v. 9)
Jesus wants us to bask in his love—to enjoy it, to permit it to motivate us, to inspire us, to reassure us.

"I have told you this so that my joy might be in you . . ." (v. 11)
There can be no more satisfying joy than the awareness of the unbounded love which the Lord has for us. It gives us a new perspective on life.

"No one has greater love than this, to lay down one's life for one's friends." (v. 13)
The very next day Jesus proved the truth of this statement by willingly laying down his life for us.

"You are my friends if you do what I command you." (v. 14)
When we are motivated by love, we will want to do whatever is pleasing to the person we love. Jesus' love for the Father moved him to fulfill every detail of the Father's will.

Jesus Prays for Us

Orientation. This last discourse of Jesus ends with a priestly prayer for all of us. It is gratifying to know that the prayer of Jesus is always answered. Love always seeks a closeness, a union with the beloved. If this is true of human love, how much greater is the desire of divine love.

Scriptural Passage for Prayer. Listen to Jesus' fervent plea:

"I pray not only for them, but also for those who will believe in me through their word, so that they may all be one, as you, Father, are in me and I in you, that they also may be in us, that the world may believe that you sent me. . . . Father, they are your gift to me. I wish that where I am they also may be with me, that they may see my glory that you gave me, because you loved me before the foundation of the world." **Jn 17:20-21, 24**

Reflections. Jesus continues to pray in these same words today. This union of love, for which Jesus prayed, is the prelude to our eternal and total union with the Holy Trinity in a bond of perfect love. This is our destiny.

In this prayer Jesus also pleads for our eternal salvation. Surely this is the desire of every one of us. What comfort in knowing that

Jesus wants our eternal happiness more than we could want it ourselves.

In this final discourse Jesus reveals himself as a concerned, unselfish, sensitive, reassuring, forgiving, healing, compassionate, generous, gracious, gentle, and, above all, loving God.

He is awaiting our response.

Moving Out of Prayer

Thank Jesus for his tender loving concern as revealed in this Last Discourse. In your journal note the aspect of Jesus' loving concern which impressed you most.

Texts for Additional Days of Prayer

You may wish to spend additional prayer time on some of the words of Jesus in this Last Discourse which have not been used in this presentation.

John 13:31-35:	"I give you a new commandment, love one another...." (v. 34)
John 14, 15, 16, and 17 contain 117 verses:	Let them lead you to passages with which you wish to pray for additional days of prayer.

NINETEEN

The Agony of Jesus in the Garden

He was in such agony and he prayed so fervently that his sweat became like drops of blood falling on the ground. **Lk 22:44**

Orientation

As we approach Jesus in the Garden of Gethsemane, we do so with awe and reverence. In his agony, Jesus suffered all the pain and distress which any one of us will ever have to endure. He saw that in many cases, his suffering would be futile because men and women would reject his offer of salvation. The dreadful fear of what lay ahead wracked his whole being. He experienced the rejection, the loneliness, the awful disgrace of dying the most shameful and painful death administered at that time—death by crucifixion. The denial by Peter, the betrayal by Judas, and the desertion by all the apostles pierced his heart.

Jesus endured an intense struggle to do his Father's will. It was the greatest human decision ever to be made. Tertullian says "No one who has not been tempted can enter the kingdom of heaven."

Scriptural Passage for Prayer

In the spirit enter the Garden of Gethsemane with Jesus. Stay close to him as the words of the Gospel find a home in your heart.

Then Jesus came with them to a place called Gethsemane, and he said to his disciples, "Sit here while I go over there and pray." He took along Peter and the two sons of Zebedee, and began to feel sorrow and distress. Then he said to them, "My soul is sorrowful even to death. Remain here and keep watch with me." He advanced a little and fell prostrate in prayer, saying, "My Father, if it is possible, let this cup pass from me; yet, not as I will, but as you will." When he returned to his disciples he found them asleep. He said to Peter, "So you could not keep watch with me for one hour? Watch and pray that you may not undergo the test. The spirit is willing, but the flesh is weak." Withdrawing a second time, he prayed again, "My Father, if it is not possible that this cup pass without my drinking it, your will be done!" Then he returned once more and found them asleep, for they could not keep their eyes open. He left them and withdrew again and prayed a third time, saying the same thing again. Then he returned to his disciples and said to them, "Are you still sleeping and taking your rest? Behold, the hour is at hand when the Son of Man is to be handed over to sinners. Get up, let us go. Look, my betrayer is at hand."

While he was still speaking, Judas, one of the Twelve, arrived, accompanied by a large crowd, with swords and clubs, who had come from the chief priests and the elders of the people. His betrayer had arranged a sign with them, saying, "The man I shall kiss is the one; arrest him." Immediately he went over to Jesus and said, "Hail, Rabbi!" and he kissed him. Jesus answered him, "Friend, do what you have come for." Then stepping forward they laid hands on Jesus and arrested him. And behold, one of those who accompanied Jesus put his hand to his sword, drew it, and struck the high priest's servant, cutting off his ear. Then Jesus said to him, "Put your sword back into its sheath, for all who take the sword will perish by the sword. Do you think that I cannot call upon my Father and he will not provide me at this moment with more than twelve legions of angels? But then how would the scriptures be fulfilled which say that it must come to pass in this way?" At that hour Jesus said to the crowds, "Have you come out as against a robber, with swords and clubs to seize me? Day after day I sat teaching in the temple area, yet you did not arrest me. But all this has come to pass that the writings of the prophets may be fulfilled." Then all the disciples left him and fled. Mt 26:36-56

Reflections

"Remain here and keep watch with me." (v. 38)
Jesus sought human comfort and consolation, but they were denied him. He turned to his Father in prayer. Prayer is a loving relationship with our Father in heaven. It was in prayer that Jesus was able to accept the will of the Father. The Father was asking him for a total act of love that would be reparation for the rejection of the Father's love by sin down through the ages. Jesus' death was his love-offering to the Father for us.

". . . not as I will, but as you will." (v. 39)
These words in the Greek are exactly the same words used in the Lord's Prayer in Matthew 6:10: "Your will be done."

. . . he found them asleep. . . . (v. 40)
The apostles did not understand what was happening. They could not comprehend the passion and death of Jesus, even though he had foretold it on three separate occasions. Jesus asked them to pray that the Spirit might enlighten them on the nature of his redemptive mission, but they fell asleep.

"Get up, let us go. . . ." (v. 46)
Jesus did not try to escape. He courageously went to meet his captors. This fulfilled what he said earlier: "I lay down my life . . . I lay it down on my own" (Jn 10:17-18).

. . . "Hail, Rabbi!" and he kissed him. Jesus answered him, "Friend, . . ." (vv. 49-50)
In spite of Judas' treachery, Jesus called him friend. Sin is a betrayal of Jesus' love for us, but he still calls us "friend." Try to experience the pain which Jesus endured in this betrayal.

Then all the disciples left him and fled. (v. 56)
Jesus' eyes must have followed them as they fled into the darkness of the night. Imagine the loneliness which gripped his

heart. He still sees his creatures fleeing into the darkness of sin. Do I flee from Jesus when he asks too much?

Moving Out of Prayer

Sit quietly and let the experience of all that transpired in the garden lead you into a fervent "thank you." Only your own heart can tell you what you should note in your journal.

Texts for Additional Days of Prayer

Matthew 26:47-56:	Jesus is betrayed, arrested, deserted.
Luke 22:39-53:	..."Why are you sleeping?..." (v. 46)
Hebrews 5:1-10:	"... he became the source of eternal salvation for all who obey him." (v. 9)
Psalm 55:13-15:	"If an enemy had reviled me, I could have borne it; ..." (v. 13)
Matthew 16:21-23:	"... Jesus began to show his disciples that he must go to Jerusalem and suffer greatly ..." (v. 21)

TWENTY

Trials of Jesus, Scourging, Crowning with Thorns

> ... Upon him was the chastisement
> that makes us whole,
> by his stripes we were healed. **Is 53:5**

Introduction

To appreciate Jesus' condemnation, scourging, and crowning with thorns, it would be fruitful to read the whole account in Matthew 26:57-75 and 27:1-31. This is too lengthy a passage to quote in its entirety here. As you read reflectively and prayerfully, you may wish to underline a word or mark a phrase or verse to which you wish to return for your prayer. Here I have provided three sections for reflection and listening prayer.

Orientation

When we contemplate the horrible suffering of Jesus, we must remember that Jesus is not a helpless victim of his captors, but one who willingly accepted this dreadful disgrace and pain to make a supreme act of love to the Father on our behalf. This is what he meant when he said: "No one has greater love than this, to lay down one's life for one's friends" (Jn 15:13).

In our prayer we now enter more deeply into a great mystery, a mystery which baffles us, a mystery whose depth we cannot fathom. It is the mystery of Jesus being judged, condemned, and sentenced by his own creatures.

Let us relive with the risen Jesus this travesty of justice, seeing with him the perfidy of the human heart. Let us stand close to him and listen as he is arraigned before the high priest. Let us go with him to the judgment seats of Pilate, then to Herod, then back to Pilate again.

Jesus Before The Sanhedrin

Scriptural Passage for Prayer.

> Those who had arrested Jesus led him away to Caiaphas the high priest, where the scribes and the elders were assembled. Peter was following him at a distance as far as the high priest's courtyard, and going inside he sat down with the servants to see the outcome. The chief priests and the entire Sanhedrin kept trying to obtain false testimony against Jesus in order to put him to death, but they found none, though many false witnesses came forward. Finally two came forward who stated, "This man said, 'I can destroy the temple of God and within three days rebuild it.'" The high priest rose and addressed him, "Have you no answer? What are these men testifying against you?" But Jesus was silent. Then the high priest said to him, "I order you to tell us under oath before the living God whether you are the Messiah, the Son of God." Jesus said to him in reply, "You have said so. But I tell you:
>
> From now on you will see 'the Son of Man
>   seated at the right hand of the Power'
>   and 'coming on the clouds of heaven.'"
>
> Then the high priest tore his robes and said, "He has blasphemed! What further need have we of witnesses? You have now heard the blasphemy; what is your opinion?" They said in reply, "He deserves to die!" Then they spat in his face

and struck him, while some slapped him, saying, "Prophesy for us, Messiah: who is it that struck you?" Mt 26:57-68

Reflections.

. . . led him away to Caiaphas . . . (v. 57)
Bringing Jesus to trial to the Sanhedrin, the supreme court of the Jews, violated almost every law governing the conduct of the affairs by this ruling body. They were driven by hatred and frenzy to get rid of Jesus without any delay.

The chief priests and the entire Sanhedrin kept trying to obtain false testimony against Jesus in order to put him to death, . . . (v. 59)
It required at least two witnesses be interviewed separately to formulate any charge against a supposed offender. Not even those testifying falsely could reach an agreement. Such was the hypocrisy and injustice of this mock trial.

. . . "I order you to tell us under oath before the living God whether you are the Messiah, the Son of God." (v. 63)
This was the clinching argument which they were seeking. If Jesus said no, he could have walked out of that courtroom a free person. His yes meant his death for blasphemy. He was crucified for telling the truth.

Jesus Before Pilate

Scriptural Passage for Prayer.

Now Jesus stood before the governor, and he questioned him, "Are you the king of the Jews?" Jesus said, "You say so." And when he was accused by the chief priests and elders, he made no answer. Then Pilate said to him, "Do you not hear how many things they are testifying against you?" But he did not answer him one word, so that the governor was greatly amazed.

Mt 27:11-14

Reflections.

. . . "Are you the king of the Jews?" . . . (v. 11)
In order to formulate a charge against Jesus, the Sanhedrin

settled on two false accusations. Jesus was going to destroy their temple and Jesus was guilty of blasphemy. However, they knew that these charges of religious insurrection would not interest the Roman governor, who would probably dismiss the case.

When they arrived at the praetorium, they trumped up another charge to bring before Pilate. They accused Jesus of calling himself the king of the Jews. This charge would capture Pilate's attention. The title "king of the Jews" was given to several Messiah pretenders who had arisen and promised to deliver their nation from Roman domination. Pilate had quickly eliminated these men and their followers as a threat to Roman rule.

... *"My kingdom does not belong to this world...."* (Jn 18:36)
Jesus immediately dispelled Pilate's fears when he made this statement. Pilate had already surmised that this was a trumped up charge since Jesus did not react like any "Messiah pretender." He was aware that the Jewish leaders delivered him up out of envy.

... *he did not answer him one word, so that the governor was greatly amazed.* (v. 14)
One of the unusual and surprising features of the trials of Jesus was the fact that he made no attempt to defend himself. When the false accusations were flung in his face, Jesus remained silent, so much so that Pilate was greatly amazed. The only response he did make was to the questions his judges had a right to ask.

At first we may conclude that Jesus realized all too well that they would twist and turn his words to formulate some kind of charge against him. While this is true, it was not the primary reason for Jesus' silence. That silence forced his judges and accusers to look inward and admit to themselves how ridiculously false were their concocted charges. Jesus was really reaching out in love, hoping to win them, not to avoid his death, but for their own salvation. In our daily lives such silence can be golden. It has a hidden power.

Scourging and Crowning

Scriptural Passage for Prayer.

Then the soldiers of the governor took Jesus inside the praetorium and gathered the whole cohort around him. They stripped off his clothes and threw a scarlet military cloak about him. Weaving a crown out of thorns, they placed it on his head, and a reed in his right hand. And kneeling before him, they mocked him, saying, "Hail, King of Jews!" They spat upon him and took the reed and kept striking him on the head. And when they had mocked him, they stripped him of the cloak, dressed him in his own clothes, and led him off to crucify him. Mt 27:27-31

Reflections.

. . . "Hail, King of the Jews!" (v. 29)
In the convent of the Ecce Homo in Jerusalem, maintained by the Sisters of Sion, there is a large flagstone. It is believed to be the "king's game" which the soldiers used to determine how they were going to mock and ridicule a prisoner who was convicted of inciting a mob against Rome.

We may shudder at what the soldiers did, but we cannot cast too many aspersions on them because they were the cohort which Pilate brought from his residence in Caesarea as a bodyguard. They did not know Jesus, and there was no personal hatred in their hearts. They considered Jesus as a deluded Galilean going to the cross.

We who know Jesus have the potential to mock him by our sinfulness. How much greater would be our offense!

Then Pilate took Jesus and had him scourged. (Jn 19:1)
When a person was condemned to death by crucifixion, he was first beaten and scourged with whips which often had pieces of bone, metal, or glass attached to them which lacerated the skin. This scourging was intended to weaken the person so that he could not resist as he was being crucified. His body was often one massive, open wound. Many prisoners died in the process.

Jesus submitted to this inhuman torture as a consequence of our sin. Only love could have motivated him to endure such savage and cruel treatment.

Moving Out of Prayer

Whisper a quiet "Thank you, Jesus" many times. In your journal write a personal note to Jesus telling him how grateful you are. Also express your sorrow for the share you had in his dreadful sufferings.

Texts for Additional Days of Prayer

Isaiah 52:13-15 and 53:1-12:	Jesus' suffering is foretold in detail eight hundred years before it took place.
Other rejections: Luke 4:14-30:	"They rose up, drove him out of the town, . . ." (v. 29)
John 6:66-71:	"As a result of this, many of his disciples returned to their former way of life . . ." (v. 66)
Psalm 22:7-11:	"But I am a worm, not a man; the scorn of men, despised by the people." (v. 7)

TWENTY-ONE

Jesus Carries His Cross and Is Crucified

... They ... led him off to crucify him. **Mt 27:31**

Introduction

The Way of the Cross is one of the first devotions which sprang up in the infant church. The early Christians would retrace the steps which Jesus walked on that painful way to Calvary. They would pause at each station to reflect on what took place at that spot.

In the traditional Way of the Cross, nine of the events were mentioned in Scripture, while the other five have come down to us from tradition. There is also a scriptural Way of the Cross approved by Pope Paul VI, which begins with the Last Supper and concludes with the resurrection.

The Way of the Cross

Orientation. In making the Way of the Cross contemplatively, you may wish to walk with Jesus, supporting and thanking him as he painfully struggles on. You may wish to accompany Mary and let her share with you as you trudge along together. You may also select one or more of your favorite stations and rest there with the Lord in a listening posture.

Scriptural Passage for Prayer.

> And when they had mocked him, they stripped him of the cloak, dressed him in his own clothes, and led him off to crucify him. As they were going out, they met a Cyrenian named Simon; this man they pressed into service to carry his cross. Mt 27:31-32

Reflections. As you move along this sorrowful path, permit your external senses to help you create an atmosphere for prayer. Listen to the derision and the scoffing hurled at Jesus by his enemies. Smell the open sewer down the center of the street with all the accumulation of garbage discarded from the many shops. Observe the frenzy of his enemies, the suspicious glances of the Roman soldiers as they guard their prisoner, the indifference of the shop owners as they huckster their wares, the tearful eyes and sad faces of Jesus' faithful followers. Support the arm of Mary, protect her from the curious crowd pressing against her.

After this prayer-walk in spirit, our own cross will seem much lighter.

Crucifixion

Orientation. Death by crucifixion was the most shameful and painful kind of execution practiced at that time. The victim died of exhaustion and asphyxiation when he became so weakened that he could not raise his head to breathe.

Crucifixion brought utter disgrace to the victim and his family. He was an outcast from society. The Romans always crucified their prisoners in conspicuous places so that the populace would not dare to defy or demonstrate against the Roman government.

Crucifixion was such a disgrace and so painful that no Roman citizen could be crucified. St. Peter was crucified, while St. Paul, a Roman citizen, was beheaded.

Scriptural Passage for Prayer.

> And when they came to a place called Golgotha (which means Place of the Skull), they gave Jesus wine to drink mixed with gall. But when he had tasted it, he refused to drink. After they

had crucified him, they divided his garments by casting lots; then they sat down and kept watch over him there. And they placed over his head the written charge against him: This is Jesus, the King of the Jews. Two revolutionaries were crucified with him, one on his right and the other on his left. Those passing by reviled him, shaking their heads and saying, "You who would destroy the temple and rebuild it in three days, save yourself, if you are the Son of God, [and] come down from the cross!" Likewise the chief priests with the scribes and elders mocked him and said, "He saved others; he cannot save himself. So he is the king of Israel! Let him come down from the cross now, and we will believe in him. He trusted in God; let him deliver him now if he wants him. For he said, 'I am the Son of God.'" The revolutionaries who were crucified with him also kept abusing him in the same way. Mt 27:33-44

Reflections.

... This is Jesus, the King of the Jews. (v. 37)
This inscription on the cross, "King of the Jews," was a sign of ridicule, since all those who rose up against the Roman occupation were labeled "King of the Jews."

Two revolutionaries were crucified with him, ... (v. 38)
This fact is the fulfillment of the prophecy of Isaiah: "he ... was counted among the wicked" (Is 53:12).

Those passing by reviled him, shaking their heads ... (v. 39)
Again the prophecy of Isaiah 53:3 is fulfilled: "He was spurned and avoided by men ..."

St. Luke records Jesus' reaction to all this infamous treatment. In spite of the derision, mockery, insults, and blasphemy hurled at Jesus, his voice came loud and clear over this whole cacophony of scorn: "Father, forgive them, they know not what they do" (Lk 23:34). Jesus not only prayed for them and us, but he even excused them and us. Such is the indomitable love of our Redeemer.

Jesus took on the consequences of our sinfulness and redeemed us by fulfilling the Father's will in an act of perfect love. Jesus

130 / The Son Redeems Us

embraced the will of the Father, not the pain of crucifixion. Sin is a rejection of God's love. Jesus offered God a perfect and an infinite act of love to repair the breach caused by man's rejection of God's love. By his incarnation and redemption, Jesus became the revelation of the Father's love to us.

When Jesus died he handed over the work of sanctification to the Holy Spirit. During our earthly sojourn, the Spirit is striving to impress upon us the truth that our sins have been forgiven.

The Death of Jesus

Scriptural Passage for Prayer. In spirit be near the cross of Jesus and listen as St. Matthew relates this deathbed scene:

> From noon onward, darkness came over the whole land until three in the afternoon. And about three o'clock Jesus cried out in a loud voice, *"Eli, Eli, lema sabachthani?"* which means, "My God, my God, why have you forsaken me?" Some of the bystanders who heard it said, "This one is calling for Elijah." Immediately one of them ran to get a sponge; he soaked it in wine, and putting it on a reed, gave it to him to drink. But the rest said, "Wait, let us see if Elijah comes to save him." But Jesus cried out again in a loud voice, and gave up his spirit. And behold, the veil of the sanctuary was torn in two from top to bottom. The earth quaked, rocks were split, tombs were opened, and the bodies of many saints who had fallen asleep were raised. And coming forth from their tombs after his resurrection, they entered the holy city and appeared to many. The centurion and the men with him who were keeping watch over Jesus feared greatly when they saw the earth quake and all that was happening, and they said, "Truly, this was the Son of God!" There were many women there, looking on from a distance, who had followed Jesus from Galilee, ministering to him. Among them were Mary Magdalene and Mary the mother of James and Joseph, and the mother of the sons of Zebedee. Mt 27:45-56

Reflections.

. . . *"My God, my God, why have you forsaken me?"* (v. 46)
Jesus could have been praying Psalm 22 with only a few words

Jesus Carries His Cross and Is Crucified / 131

being recorded by the crowd. He could have prayed the rest of the psalm quietly as a sick person may do with the Our Father.

On the other hand this could have been a lament coming straight from the heart of Jesus. Let its words reach your heart.

And behold, the veil of the sanctuary was torn in two from top to bottom.... (v. 51)
This was a sign that the old dispensation was over and Jesus had initiated the new covenant with his promise of full life.

... "Truly, this was the Son of God!" (v. 54)
The significance of this great act of faith is that the centurion, a Gentile, was the first to recognize Jesus publicly as God by his redemptive death.

There were many women there, looking on from a distance, ... (v. 55)
The presence of these devoted women brought much comfort to Jesus in his dying moments when so many others either deserted him or turned against him.

Moving Out of Prayer

Gaze long and lovingly on your crucifix. Ask the Holy Spirit to give you a deeper appreciation of the mystery of Jesus' love for us. In your journal let a word or phrase convey the sentiments in your heart.

Texts for Additional Days of Prayer

Another source of prayer to help us ponder the debasement of Jesus and his glorification is found in a very early Christian hymn which Paul incorporated into his letter to the Philippians.

Philippians 2:5-11:	"He humbled himself, becoming obedient to death, even death on a cross." (v. 8)
	Jesus reveals very much about himself in the last words he spoke from his

deathbed on the cross. These treasured words can lead us into listening prayer.

Matthew 27:46:	... "My God, my God, why have you forsaken me?"
Luke 23:34:	... "Father, forgive them, they know not what they do." ...
Luke 23:43:	..."Amen, I say to you, today you will be with me in Paradise."
Luke 23:46:	... "Father, into your hands I commend my spirit."
John 19:26-27:	... "Behold, your son ... Behold, your mother." ...
John 19:28:	... "I thirst."
John 19:30:	... "It is finished."

TWENTY-TWO

Jesus Is Taken Down From the Cross and Laid in a Tomb

A grave was assigned him among the wicked and a burial place with evil doers, . . . **Is 53:9**

Burial of Jesus

Orientation. In your prayer, stand with Mary Magdalene and the other Mary close to the tomb. It is quiet now as evening approaches: no more gloating, no more raucous cries of blasphemy, no more confusion fills the air. Jesus has completed his redemptive mission.

Scriptural Passage for Prayer. St. Matthew records the event calmly and factually:

> When it was evening, there came a rich man from Arimathea named Joseph, who was himself a disciple of Jesus. He went to Pilate and asked for the body of Jesus; then Pilate ordered it to be handed over. Taking the body, Joseph wrapped it [in] clean linen and laid it in his new tomb that he had hewn in the rock. Then he rolled a huge stone across the entrance to the tomb and departed. But Mary Magdalene and the other Mary remained sitting there, facing the tomb. **Mt 27:57-61**

Reflections.

. . . there came a rich man from Arimathea named Joseph, . . . (v. 57)
Joseph was a dedicated disciple. It took courage to go to Pilate to ask for the body of Jesus. Pilate was exhausted and disgusted with the Jews in forcing his hand to execute Jesus. Joseph risked Pilate's ire.

Joseph was most gracious and generous. He had hewn a tomb for himself in the rock which he gladly gave to Jesus, trusting that he himself would not need a tomb in the near future. Remember the Jews were buried immediately after death. There could have been little time to obtain another tomb. Joseph's love for Jesus removed all fear or anxiety about that.

But Mary Magdalene and the other Mary remained sitting there, facing the tomb. (v. 61)
These holy women followed Jesus through thick and thin. They journeyed with him, took care of his needs and that of the apostles. They were faithful in supporting him during his dreadful condemnation and death. Now their devotion and dedication prompted them to remain close to him in death.

The Guard at the Tomb

Scriptural Passage for Prayer. St. Matthew reveals the grave doubts and fears in the minds of his enemies, even though they saw Jesus die on the cross:

> The next day, the one following the day of preparation, the chief priests and the Pharisees gathered before Pilate and said, "Sir, we remember that this imposter while still alive said, 'After three days I will be raised up.' Give orders, then, that the grave be secured until the third day, lest his disciples come and steal him and say to the people, 'He has been raised from the dead.' This last imposture would be worse than the first." Pilate said to them, "The guard is yours; go secure it as best you can." So they went and secured the tomb by fixing a seal to the stone and setting the guard. Mt 27:62-66

Reflections.

"Give orders, then, that the grave be secured..." (v. 64)

This incident may cause us to wonder if the chief priests and Pharisees may have feared that there was a possibility of Jesus rising from the dead. They remembered that he had power over life and death.

How often human beings have tried to thwart the plans of God! Hatred and lack of faith are so blinding to the ways of God. Have we found ourselves closed or reluctant to listen to the inspirations of grace? The Lord never forces us, but he waits.

The Sufferings of Jesus' Mother Mary

Scriptural Passage for Prayer.

Standing by the cross of Jesus were his mother and his mother's sister, Mary the wife of Clopas, and Mary of Magdala. **Jn 19:25**

Reflections.

Standing by the cross of Jesus were his mother... (v. 25)

In his Gospel, John tells us that Mary, Jesus' mother, was standing by the cross. In prayer, be with Mary at this crucial time.

When Jesus finally handed over his life to the Father, it must have been a moment of great relief for his mother. When Jesus uttered "It is finished," his mother must have welcomed the end of his tortuous suffering. Now her Son was released from his agony. He had given over his life to the Father. And suddenly the world was empty. It was cold, cruel, and forbidding for this mother who dearly loved her Son.

The pain of separation was not new to Mary. She experienced it many times: the flight into Egypt, the loss of Jesus in the temple at the age of twelve, Jesus' departure from the family home at Nazareth to begin his ministry.

Standing here in the shadow of the cross, Mary did find some consolation in the loving concern of Joseph of Arimathea and

Nicodemus who gently prepared Jesus' body for burial.

Mary was greatly gratified to witness the love and loyalty to her Son of the holy women who courageously stood beside him throughout his bitter suffering and death. Even in death they did not leave him. "Mary Magdalene and the other Mary remained sitting there, facing the tomb" (Mt 27:61).

Surely Mary's pain was lessened by the empathy and sorrow of the apostles when she returned to the Upper Room. As there were no words of bitterness on Mary's lips as she stood by the cross of Jesus, nor were there any incriminations of the apostles who deserted him.

Remain close to Mary during this long day while Jesus lay in the tomb.

As we contemplate the emptiness, the void, the aloneness which Mary felt in losing her Son in death, it will bring us to a greater appreciation of the treasure which is ours. Our prayer at the tomb will deepen our own appreciation for this tremendous gift.

Moving Out of Prayer

Spend some time all alone at the tomb of Jesus. Visualize what life would be like without his personal presence in the Eucharist—without his forgiving, healing love in the Sacrament of Reconciliation—without his abiding presence with us at every moment of the day.

In your journal list some of the virtues which Jesus manifested throughout his passion and death. Such a listing can have a transforming power on your mind, heart, and soul.

Texts for Additional Days of Prayer

As you linger in spirit with Mary at the tomb of Jesus, ponder the many occasions when she endured pain and suffering. Probably her greatest sorrow was the rejection which Jesus was receiving. You may wish to contemplate one of the following incidents:

Matthew 1:18-25:	"Joseph . . . decided to divorce her quietly." (v. 19)
Matthew 2:13-15:	". . . Rise, take the child and his mother, flee to Egypt, . . ." (v. 13)
Luke 2:41-52:	". . . Son, why have you done this to us? . . ." (v. 48)
Luke 8:19-21:	. . . "My mother and my brothers are those who hear the word of God and act on it." (v. 21)
John 19:25-27:	"Standing by the cross of Jesus were his mother and his mother's sister, Mary . . ." (v. 25)

Part Four:

The Risen Lord Sends the Spirit

PART FOUR

Introduction

IN THE FOURTH STAGE OF OUR PRAYER JOURNEY with Jesus, we focus on his resurrection from the dead and the coming of the promised Holy Spirit. In our prayer we meet Jesus in his many appearances immediately after his resurrection from the dead. His frequent appearances offer sufficient proof that he is alive and well. Repetition enables us to form an ongoing awareness of the abiding presence of the risen Jesus with us.

Resurrection does not mean resuscitation. Jesus did not rise with his physical body completely healed and revitalized. Jesus rose with a new body, a glorified body. Resurrection means a rising to a new and higher life.

Jesus now had a new look about him. Mary Magdalene was unable to recognize him until he called her by name. On the road to Emmaus the disciples did not recognize Jesus as he walked along with them. Mark says: "He appeared in another form to two of them..." (Mk 16:12).

There was an undefinable aura of unfamiliarity about Jesus as he appeared to his apostles and others, yet these encounters were very real. They caused some uneasiness, some incredulity. To his friends Jesus seemed at first to be a total stranger. He would suddenly appear and disappear just as unexpectedly. He often appeared in connection with a meal to prove he was a real person with a body.

The disciples did not have a close human intimacy with the risen Jesus. Everything about him was new. Yet Jesus inspired a deep peace, a confident trust, and a firm faith in the hearts of all. Jesus was teaching his disciples and us that his risen and glorified presence with us is very real, though unseen. It requires faith in him and in his promises. His appearances were the genesis of apostolic faith.

After the resurrection Jesus plays a new role. He now fulfills the role of Consoler. Who would doubt or try to estimate the consolation and comfort he brought to his mother, or the peace and joy which filled Mary Magdalene as she patiently stood by him at the tomb? He brought great joy and relief to the apostles assembled in the Upper Room for fear of the Jews. He did not reproach them for their desertion of him in his hour of need. His appearance was a healing balm for them. They rejoiced at his risen presence even though they could not quite comprehend what was happening. The risen Jesus brought great peace and joy to very many, including the appearance to the "five hundred brothers" that Paul mentions in 1 Corinthians 15:6.

The risen Jesus now testifies himself that his power is universal. "All power in heaven and on earth has been given to me" (Mt 28:18). By his resurrection the kingdom of God has become a terrestrial reality as he dwells within each one of us and gives his divine life to us.

The early Christians did not long to "return" to the good old days, but they yearned for the *parousia*—his return to them. The Holy Spirit was enlightening them with a growing understanding of the significance of the death and resurrection of Jesus. They now experienced a peace and a joy which they never had before. Their faith and hope in the eternal life which awaited them inspired within them a deep love—a love they longed to translate into service of one another.

Our contemplative prayer should be completely dominated by the spirit of the risen Jesus who longs to pray with us. In silence and solitude, let us meet the risen Jesus and let our hearts respond in wonder, love, and praise.

TWENTY-THREE

The Resurrection of Jesus

... Just as Christ was raised from the dead by the glory of the Father, we too might live in newness of life. **Rom 6:4**

Prelude

On the very day of the resurrection and for forty days thereafter, Jesus appeared to many of his friends, to some individually and to others in groups.

Could there be any doubt that Jesus must have first appeared to his mother, even though Scripture does not mention this fact? It is interesting to note how St. Ignatius deals with this question in the *Spiritual Exercises*:

> "He appeared to the Virgin Mary. Though this is not mentioned explicitly in Scripture, it must be considered as stated when Scripture says that he appeared to many others. For Scripture supposes that we have understanding, as it is written, 'Are you also without understanding?'" (*Spiritual Exercises*, No. 299)

None of us would dare to invade the privacy of that meeting, even if it were possible. We can well imagine the outpouring of love between Jesus and his mother. Her rejoicing in his great victory continues in heaven today.

Orientation

The many appearances of Jesus to different people proves that he is truly alive and well. Jesus had an even greater reason for permitting so many to see him in his risen form. He came as a Consoler and he was bringing great peace and joy, comfort and consolation, to his friends and loved ones. His appearances strengthened their faith beyond any fear or doubt. It became a dynamic, operative faith as they endeavored to live his way of life.

Scriptural Passage for Prayer

After the sabbath, as the first day of the week was dawning, Mary Magdalene and the other Mary came to see the tomb. And behold, there was a great earthquake; for an angel of the Lord descended from heaven, approached, rolled back the stone, and sat upon it. His appearance was like lightning and his clothing was white as snow. The guards were shaken with fear of him and became like dead men. Then the angel said to the women in reply, "Do not be afraid! I know that you are seeking Jesus the crucified. He is not here, for he has been raised just as he said. Come and see the place where he lay. Then go quickly and tell his disciples, 'He has been raised from the dead, and he is going before you to Galilee; there you will see him.' Behold, I have told you." Then they went away quickly from the tomb, fearful yet overjoyed, and ran to announce this to his disciples. And behold, Jesus met them on their way and greeted them. They approached, embraced his feet, and did him homage. Then Jesus said to them, "Do not be afraid. Go tell my brothers to go to Galilee, and there they will see me." **Mt 28:1-10**

Reflections

... as the first day of the week was dawning, ... (v. 1)
The resurrection of Jesus, the coming of the Holy Spirit, and other important events in the Christian era took place on the first day of the week. For this reason the Church has designated Sunday as the Lord's Day.

. . . Mary Magdalene and the other Mary came to see the tomb. (v. 1)
The love of these holy women for Jesus manifested itself in their loyalty and devotion to him, even though his life and mission seemed to end in shame, disgrace, and defeat.

. . . "Do not be afraid! . . ." (v. 5)
Any time there is an obvious intervention of the Lord in the life of anyone, there is always an invitation not to be afraid. When the Lord is active in our lives, we will experience some fear and reluctance accompanied by peace and joy.

". . . for he has been raised just as he said. . . ." (v. 6)
These dedicated women were the first to hear the good news of the resurrection. They were also the first delegated to inform the other disciples. The Lord always chooses willing hearts to accomplish his plan.

And behold, Jesus met them on their way . . . (v. 9)
The women were doing the angel's bidding, which was the will of the Lord. Seeing Jesus was their reward for their willing service and obedience. As we strive to fulfill the Lord's will in our daily commitment to our duties, we can be certain that Jesus is with us. He may even make his presence felt in order to encourage and assist us.

. . . "Do not be afraid. Go and tell my brothers . . ." (v. 10)
Once again Jesus reminds us not to be afraid when he asks us to carry out some task or mission. The women might have hesitated momentarily since the disciples might think that they were deluded and had not really seen Jesus. When Jesus says, "Don't be afraid" to them and to us, he is really saying: "Trust me."

Jesus told the father of the boy with a demon: "Everything is possible to one who has faith." With the boy's father let us pray: "I do believe, help my unbelief!" (Mk 9:23-24).

Moving Out of Prayer

Rest in the sunshine of the Lord radiant in his glorified life. Let your heart repeat Alleluia, Alleluia. . . .

In your journal you may wish to thank the Lord for the glorious resurrection which is awaiting you when you will receive his divine life in all its splendor.

Texts for Additional Days of Prayer

Colossians 3:1-4:	"If then you were raised with Christ, seek what is above ..." (v. 1)
Romans 6:3-11:	"We shall also be united with him in the resurrection...." (v. 5)
John 11:21-27:	... "I am the resurrection and the life; ..." (v. 25)
Romans 8:11-13:	"... the one who raised Christ from the dead will give life to your mortal bodies also, through his Spirit that dwells in you."(v. 11)
Ephesians 2:4-10:	"For by grace you have been saved through faith, ..." (v. 8)

TWENTY-FOUR

Jesus Appears to Mary Magdalene and the Disciples

... "I am the resurrection and the life; whoever believes in me, even if he dies, will live." **Jn 11:25**

Introduction

The resurrection of Jesus from the dead is the most important feast of the liturgy of the church. It is also the greatest event in salvation history. Throughout his whole public life, Jesus prepared his followers for his resurrection even though they did not quite understand what he meant. He promised that he would not leave us orphans, but would come back to remain with us.

Why Did Jesus Rise? By rising from the dead Jesus set the seal of approval on his claims to be the Son of God and also confirmed the message he had taught. He promised that he would willingly give up his life for our redemption, but that he would rise again.

All the promises and prophecies, all the prayers and expectations, of the Old Testament were fulfilled in his rising from the dead. Furthermore, Jesus promised that we, too, would rise with him.

We find great joy, peace, and reassurance in the resurrection of Jesus knowing that we, too, will rise and will be happy with him for all eternity.

There is another important reason why Jesus rose from the dead. Jesus loves us with an infinite love. Love always wants a close relationship with the beloved. Jesus loves us so much he could not separate himself from us. Through his resurrection, he created a new and risen life which he shared with us. He dwells with us and within us. St. Augustine says: "He is closer to me than my inmost being."

Jesus promised this close union with him and the Father: "Whoever loves me will keep my word, and my Father will love him, and we will come to him and make our dwelling with him" (Jn 14:23). Jesus prayed fervently for this intimate union with him: "So that they may all be one, as you, Father, are in me and I in you, that they also may be in us" (Jn 17:21).

There are two recorded appearances of Jesus on the day of the resurrection: the first to Mary Magdalene; the second to the disciples in the Upper Room. Either one of these is ample food for your prayer time. Choose the one to which the Holy Spirit seems to be leading you.

Appearance to Mary Magdalene

Orientation. When Jesus appeared to Mary Magdalene on the day of the resurrection he was already fulfilling his role as Consoler. Mary Magdalene was grieving over her loss of the person who loved her dearly. Jesus was always eager to heal pain and sorrow. With a listening heart, let us become a part of the scene of this sacred meeting:

Scriptural Passage for Prayer.

> But Mary stayed outside the tomb weeping. And as she wept, she bent over into the tomb and saw two angels in white sitting there, one at the head and one at the feet where the body of Jesus had been. And they said to her, "Woman, why are you weeping?" She said to them, "They have taken my Lord, and I

don't know where they laid him." When she had said this, she turned around and saw Jesus there, but did not know it was Jesus. Jesus said to her, "Woman, why are you weeping? Whom are you looking for?" She thought it was the gardener and said to him, "Sir, if you carried him away, tell me where you laid him, and I will take him." Jesus said to her, "Mary!" She turned and said to him in Hebrew, "Rabbouni," which means Teacher. Jesus said to her, "Stop holding on to me, for I have not yet ascended to the Father. But go to my brothers and tell them, 'I am going to my Father and your Father, to my God and your God.'" Mary of Magdala went and announced to the disciples, "I have seen the Lord," and what he told her. Jn 20:11-18

Reflections.

. . . and saw two angels in white sitting there, . . . (v. 12)
Mary is mystified by the appearance of these heavenly beings, but her sorrow at the loss of Jesus overwhelms her. Nothing can compare with his love.

. . . "They have taken away my Lord, . . ." (v. 13)
Even though Mary believed that Jesus was dead, she still wanted to anoint and reverence his body. She was dismayed at what might have happened to the tomb; it was empty even though she witnessed his being laid to rest and the tomb sealed.

. . . "Sir, if you carried him away, tell me where you laid him, and I will take him." (v. 15)
Love knows no limits. Mary did not realize that she could never have carried the body of Jesus, but that did not deter her. She wanted to be close to him even in death.

Jesus said to her, "Mary!" . . . (v. 16)
When Jesus called her "woman", she did not recognize his voice, but when he called her by name she immediately knew him. We are flattered when people call us by name, because it bespeaks of a good relationship with that person. Our loving Father tells us: "I have called you by name: you are mine" (Is 43:1). And Jesus said that his sheep would recognize his voice (Jn 10).

... *"I have seen the Lord,"* ... (v. 18)

Jesus first entrusted to Mary Magdalene the joyful news of his resurrection. Her announcement, "I have seen the Lord," sounded too good to be true to his disciples. These words ushered in the "new creation" which the Lord had promised.

Appearance to the Disciples

Orientation. By his death and resurrection, Jesus restored our relationship with the Father, which had been severed when sin entered the world. His redemption was universal. It included every human being who lived or who would ever live.

Jesus knew that his redemption's universality might cause us to wonder or doubt at times if we were also included in it. For this reason Jesus personalized his forgiving, healing love when he instituted the Sacrament of Reconciliation and empowered his apostles to dispense his forgiveness through this rite. This is the import of his first meeting with the apostles on the day of the resurrection. Let us listen with our hearts.

Scriptural Passage for Prayer.

> On the evening of that first day of the week, when the doors were locked, where the disciples were, for fear of the Jews, Jesus came and stood in their midst and said to them, "Peace be with you." When he had said this, he showed them his hands and his side. The disciples rejoiced when they saw the Lord. [Jesus] said to them again, "Peace be with you. As the Father has sent me, so I send you." And when he had said this, he breathed on them and said to them, "Receive the holy Spirit. Whose sins you forgive are forgiven them, and whose sins you retain are retained." **Jn 20:19-23**

Reflections.

... *"Peace be with you."* (v. 19)

The word of peace which Jesus used is *shalom*. This means much more than the one word peace. It is a prayerful wish for the sum total of all God's blessings. This kind of peace is the fruit of a good relationship with God our Father, with ourselves, with our neighbor, and with all of creation.

... *"Receive the holy Spirit...."* (v. 23)
This is the first Pentecost. The outpouring of his Spirit upon the apostles would empower them to forgive sins in his name. The work of sanctification now belongs to the Holy Spirit.

... *"Whose sins you forgive are forgiven them, ..."* (v. 23)
In these words Jesus instituted the Sacrament of Reconciliation and empowered his first priests to administer his forgiving, healing love in this sacrament, thus assuring the peace—the *shalom*—which he had come to give us.

Forgiveness of sin is the only pathway to a good relationship with God our Father and others.

Moving Out of Prayer

Repeat a word or phrase slowly and softly, such as "My Lord and my God!"

Don't neglect your journal entry. Record what the risen Christ is saying to you.

Texts for Additional Days of Prayer

Continuing this theme of prayer will keep you more and more aware of the abiding presence of the risen Jesus with you.

John 10:17-18:	"... I lay down my life in order to take it up again." (v. 17)
John 14:23:	"... We will come to him and make our dwelling with him."
Luke 24:36-49:	... "Peace be with you." (v. 36)
John 20:24-29:	... "My Lord and my God." (v. 28)
Galatians 2:19-21:	"... I live, no longer I, but Christ lives in me; ..." (v. 20)

TWENTY-FIVE

The Appearance on the Road to Emmaus

After this he appeared in another form to two of them walking along on their way to the country. **Mk 16:12**

Orientation

For many people the account of what took place on the road to Emmaus is by far their favorite post-resurrection appearance of Jesus. We can more easily identify with the two disciples as they journeyed along. Like them, we often have difficulty understanding the true nature and mission of the Messiah. It is hard for us to understand why we must walk the way of the cross before entering into glory.

Throughout our whole life, there is a constant striving to keep ourselves ever aware that we are living with the risen Jesus. He is our transcendent God, but also a very immanent God, walking with us as we begin anew our daily trek to our own Emmaus.

We have much in common with these two disciples of Jesus. They were hurting. They were fearful. On that black Friday all their aspirations, hopes, and dreams had been totally shattered as their Messiah hung exposed, mocked, ridiculed, and now dead and entombed. They had been so excited, so full of hope. The Christ of Palm Sunday had filled them with a dream of victory, but all of that came to an abrupt end.

Even though their hearts ached and the stabs of pain were excruciating, there was still a glimmer of hope. There was a power keeping them from despair. All that began to change when a stranger joined them as they slowly and listlessly moved along.

Our Daily Emmaus Journey. On our own road to Emmaus, we may have similar experiences. Doubt, fear, and anxiety may weigh heavily upon our hearts. The cross may seem insufferably heavy; the journey rough, rocky, and steep. We may be tempted to ask: "Why me, Lord? What have I done to deserve this? What's the use of going on?"

As darkness seems to increase, we may hear an inner voice whispering: "Behold, I am with you always" (Mt 28:20). "I will not leave you orphans" (Jn 14:18). "My grace is sufficient for you, for power is made perfect in weakness" (2 Cor 12:9).

Scriptural Passage for Prayer

In prayer we will soon recognize the Lord as he walks with us. As you read this lengthy passage slowly and reflectively, underscore or mark any word or phrase which may be a stepping stone for you in quiet prayer.

> Now that very day two of them were going to a village seven miles from Jerusalem called Emmaus, and they were conversing about all the things that had occurred. And it happened that while they were conversing and debating, Jesus himself drew near and walked with them, but their eyes were prevented from recognizing him. He asked them, "What are you discussing as you walk along?" They stopped, looking downcast. One of them, named Cleopas, said to him in reply, "Are you the only visitor to Jerusalem who does not know of the things that have taken place there in these days?" And he replied to them, "What sort of things?" They said to him, "The things that happened to Jesus the Nazarene, who was a prophet mighty in deed and word before God and all the people, how our chief priests and rulers both handed him over to a sentence of death and crucified him. But we were hoping that he would be the one to redeem Israel; and besides all this, it is now the third day since this took

place. Some women from our group, however, have astounded us: they were at the tomb early in the morning and did not find his body; they came back and reported that they had indeed seen a vision of angels who announced that he was alive. Then some of those with us went to the tomb and found things just as the women had described, but him they did not see." And he said to them, "Oh, how foolish you are! How slow of heart to believe all that the prophets spoke! Was it not necessary that the Messiah should suffer these things and enter into his glory?" Then beginning with Moses and all the prophets, he interpreted to them what referred to him in all the scriptures. As they approached the village to which they were going, he gave the impression that he was going on farther. But they urged him, "Stay with us, for it is nearly evening and the day is almost over." So he went in to stay with them. And it happened that, while he was with them at table, he took bread, said the blessing, broke it, and gave it to them. With that their eyes were opened and they recognized him, but he vanished from their sight. Then they said to each other, "Were not our hearts burning [within us] while he spoke to us on the way and opened the scriptures to us?" So they set out at once and returned to Jerusalem where they found gathered together the eleven and those with them who were saying, "The Lord has truly been raised and has appeared to Simon!" Then the two recounted what had taken place on the way and how he was made known to them in the breaking of the bread. Lk 24:13-35

Reflections

One of the most sublime ways in which Jesus keeps us aware of his abiding presence with us is through the Eucharist. His presence here is visible through the sign and symbol of bread and wine.

There are a number of parallels between the events on the road to Emmaus and the Sacrifice of the Mass.

". . . How slow of heart to believe all that the prophets spoke! . . ." (v. 25) Like the disciples, we may be discouraged and disheartened at

the events in our life. We may come to the Eucharist with a lack of faith and trust in the Lord. If so, at the penitential rite we ask for forgiveness and healing for our lack of faith and trust.

Then beginning with Moses and all the prophets, he interpreted to them what referred to him in all the scriptures. (v. 27)
During the Liturgy of the Word, Jesus explains his Word to us. As we listen we find inspiration and motivation. His Word has a transforming power to mold our thoughts, words, and attitudes according to his heart and mind.

... "Stay with us, for it is nearly evening and the day is almost over." (v. 29)
Note that Jesus gave the impression that he was going farther. Jesus always waits for our invitation. He never imposes himself upon us, but respects our free will. Unfortunately we, by choice, may not be open or receptive to his presence or his will for us.

... he took bread, said the blessing, broke it, and gave it to them. (v. 30)
By his eucharistic presence Jesus comforts and consoles us, forgives and heals us, inspires and motivates us, strengthens and encourages us. Above all, his presence and his coming to us proves his boundless love for us.

... "Were not our hearts burning [within us] while he spoke to us on the way and opened the scriptures to us?" (v. 32)
Jesus is present in his Word and speaks to us personally through his Word. His Word has the power to keep our hearts burning within us if we listen quietly and prayerfully to what he is communicating.

So they set out at once and returned to Jerusalem. . . . (v. 33)
The dismissal at the end of Mass, "Go in peace to love and serve the Lord," is really a commission to go forth to live his way of life so completely that we can draw others closer to him by sharing the good news of redemption with them.

Moving Out of Prayer

Gaze longingly and lovingly at Jesus as he sits with the two disciples and breaks bread with them. In your journal note your feelings at your recognition of Jesus in prayer or at some other time in your life.

Texts for Additional Days of Prayer

---

1 Peter 1:3-12:	"... who in his great mercy gave us a new birth ... through the resurrection of Jesus Christ from the dead." (v. 3)
Mark 16:12-13:	"After this he appeared in another form to two of them...." (v. 12)
Luke 24:36-49:	"... he stood in their midst ..." (v. 36)
Matthew 28:1-10:	"... Behold, Jesus met them on their way ..." (v. 9)
1 Corinthians 15:8:	"Last of all, as to one born abnormally, he appeared to me."

TWENTY-SIX

Breakfast on the Lakeshore

... "Come after me, and I will make you fishers of men." **Mk 1:17**

Introduction

The events which took place on the shore of the Sea of Galilee can be divided into two separate parts: breakfast after the astonishing catch of fish and the establishment of the primacy of St. Peter. Each section is sufficiently rich in inspiration and insights for a time of prayer.

Miraculous Catch and Breakfast

Orientation. An artist painted a picture to be placed over a large fireplace in a retreat house. His picture depicted Jesus on the lakeshore preparing the meal for his disciples. The scene is recorded in this Gospel account. As you study the artist's concept of what took place, you can see a great variety of faces appearing on the side of a hill used as a backdrop for this scene. The artist was trying to envision the countless people who would ponder this event and be moved to recognize Jesus as the loving Provider and Consoler.

In our prayer, we focus on this appearance of Jesus and what he revealed about himself. Jesus' appearance with his glorified body is another blow to those skeptics who would have us believe that the resurrection never took place.

This event also reveals Jesus as fulfilling his role as Consoler. The apostles labored all night and caught nothing. They were hungry, tired, and discouraged. Jesus came to their rescue by arranging for this huge catch of fish.

Jesus loves us with a providing love if we will only acknowledge our inability to accomplish anything without his help. The apostles admitted their poverty and only then did Jesus miraculously step in to help them. When Jesus cautioned us "without me you can do nothing" (Jn 15:5), he was teaching us that with him we can do all things. Jesus was manifesting to us his loving care and concern for us at all times.

Scriptural Passage for Prayer.

After this, Jesus revealed himself again to his disciples at the Sea of Tiberias. He revealed himself in this way. Together were Simon Peter, Thomas called Didymus, Nathanael from Cana in Galilee, Zebedee's sons, and two others of his disciples. Simon Peter said to them, "I am going fishing." They said to him, "We also will come with you." So they went out and got into the boat, but that night they caught nothing. When it was already dawn, Jesus was standing on the shore; but the disciples did not realize that it was Jesus. Jesus said to them, "Children, have you caught anything to eat?" They answered him, "No." So he said to them, "Cast the net over the right side of the boat and you will find something." So they cast it, and were not able to pull it in because of the number of fish. So the disciple whom Jesus loved said to Peter, "It is the Lord." When Simon Peter heard that it was the Lord, he tucked in his garment, for he was lightly clad, and jumped into the sea. The other disciples came in the boat, for they were not far from shore, only about a hundred yards, dragging the net with the fish. When they climbed out on shore, they saw a charcoal fire with fish on it and bread. Jesus said to them, "Bring some of the fish you just caught." So Simon Peter went over and dragged the net ashore full of one hundred fifty-three large fish. Even though there were so many, the net was not torn. Jesus said to them, "Come, have breakfast." And none of the disciples dared to ask him, "Who are you?" because they realized it was the Lord. Jesus came over and took the bread and gave it to them, and in like manner the fish. This was now the third time Jesus was revealed to his disciples after being raised from the dead. Jn 21:1-14

Reflections.

... *"Children, have you caught anything to eat?"* ... (v. 5)
The word "children" is a term of friendship and endearment. It is neither a belittling nor a derogatory expression. It is used often in Scripture.

... *"Cast the net over the right side of the boat ..."* (v. 6)
This was a blow to their professionalism. They knew how to fish and yet they had caught nothing. Who was this stranger to tell them where and how to fish? In some quarters there was a superstition which would never tolerate casting a net over the starboard side. However, the apostles were docile and followed his instructions. This was just another reminder of the Lord telling us: "For my thoughts are not your thoughts, nor are your ways my ways" (Is 55:8).

So Simon Peter went over and dragged the net ashore full of one hundred fifty-three large fish. (v. 11)
There has been much speculation about the meaning of the exact number of fish that were taken. One explanation goes so far as to maintain that there were one hundred fifty-three varieties of fish in the lake and one of each variety was caught to indicate that some day one hundred fifty-three nations of the world would be brought into the "net of Peter."
A more plausible explanation contends that already the apostles were practicing the love of neighbor—counting the fish so that each one received his just amount. If so, the proportionate dividing of the fish is a reminder to us of our duty to love one another honestly and sincerely.

Peter Called to Shepherd

Orientation. Observe the loving concern that Jesus had for Peter. He did not want to embarrass Peter before the other disciples, nor did he want Peter to bow to peer pressure. He took Peter aside to ask him about his personal love, because he wanted Peter to be honest and sincere.

Jesus always responds to the individual. He is exclusively for us when we go to him.

Scriptural Passage for Prayer. Listen intently to the exchange between Jesus and Peter. As you read the passage reflectively, ask yourself honestly how would you respond to Jesus' questions.

> When they had finished breakfast, Jesus said to Simon Peter, "Simon, son of John, do you love me more than these?" He said to him, "Yes, Lord, you know that I love you." He said to him, "Feed my lambs." He then said to him a second time, "Simon, son of John, do you love me?" He said to him, "Yes, Lord, you know that I love you." He said to him, "Tend my sheep." He said to him the third time, "Simon, son of John, do you love me?" Peter was distressed that he had said to him a third time, "Do you love me?" and he said to him, "Lord, you know everything; you know that I love you." [Jesus] said to him, "Feed my sheep. Amen, amen, I say to you, when you were younger, you used to dress yourself and go where you wanted; but when you grow old, you will stretch out your hands, and someone else will dress you and lead you where you do not want to go." He said this signifying by what kind of death he would glorify God. And when he had said this, he said to him, "Follow me." **Jn 21:15-19**

Reflections.

> ... *"Simon, son of John, do you love me more than these?"* ... (v. 15)
> We are not exactly sure what Jesus meant by "more than these." He might have been referring to his fishing or his love for the rest of the disciples with him or even more than these disciples do. There are two different words used for "love": filial love with which we love others, and agape love with which we love God. Jesus could have been trying to raise Peter's love above the human to the divine. They might also have been used as synonyms.

He said to him the third time, "Simon, son of John, do you love me?"... (v. 17)

Peter was distressed when Jesus asked the same question for the third time, but he was beginning to recognize that he could not accomplish anything on his own. Hence, he said: "Lord, you know everything . . ." This threefold confession of faith was probably meant to counteract the triple denial of Peter in the courtyard of the high priest.

... "Feed my lambs."... "Tend my sheep."... "Feed my sheep...." (vv. 15-17)

This event not only manifests Peter's reinstatement into the good graces of the Lord, but it is the occasion when Jesus conferred the primacy on Peter. In tending the sheep, Peter is now the shepherd of the flock, the church. The fact that Jesus provided this leadership for his church should fill us with much peace and joy. It means that we have a teaching authority guided by the Holy Spirit. This has guaranteed the perpetuation of the church down through the centuries.

Moving Out of Prayer

In spirit, sit on the shore of the lake and listen to the gentle splashing sound of the waves lapping on the sandy shore. As you recall what was said and done in this encounter, experience the love which flowed between Jesus and his disciples.

In your journal entry, respond to Jesus' question: "Do you love me?"

Texts for Additional Days of Prayer

Luke 5:1-11:	..."Put out into deep water and lower your nets for a catch." (v. 4)
Matthew 16:13-20:	"... You are Peter, and upon this rock I will build my church." (v. 18)
Luke 7:36-50:	"... Her many sins have been forgiven;

	hence, she has shown great love . . ." (v. 46)
Matthew 26:31-55:	". . . This very night before the cock crows, you will deny me three times." (v. 34)
Galatians 1:18-24:	". . . I went up to Jerusalem to confer with Kephas . . . (v. 18)

TWENTY-SEVEN

The Ascension of Jesus Into Heaven

"... I am going to my Father and your Father, to my God and your God." **Jn 20:17**

Orientation

The ascension of Jesus into heaven marks the formal termination of his appearances after his resurrection. The many appearances of Jesus help us to form the habit pattern of being constantly aware of his abiding presence with us in the power of the resurrection. Now he has ascended to the right hand of the Father to reign in glory and power. Habit patterns are formed by repetition. Our prayer should always be oriented to our contemporary living with the risen and glorified Jesus. He is with us here and now.

From these frequent resurrection appearances and his subsequent reign in glory, we can glean some little insights into heaven. We can be certain that it will not be a prolonged vacation, nor an honorable retirement, but a loving dynamic, operative living with Jesus in the glory of heaven.

Scriptural Passages for Prayer

St. Luke records two separate accounts of Jesus' ascension into heaven. Since the Gospel account is not lengthy, nor is it repetitive, we have combined these two accounts as a source of prayer. Hopefully, you will find a prayer word or a resting place in one of the accounts which will launch you into a deep and personal union with the Lord.

Before Jesus left this world, he formally established his church as his kingdom on earth by authorizing and commissioning the apostles to continue the mission which he inaugurated. He empowered them to dispense his divine life and love through the sacramental channels he had instituted. Then he took his leave.

> When they had gathered together they asked him, "Lord, are you at this time going to restore the kingdom to Israel?" He answered them, "It is not for you to know the times or seasons that the Father has established by his own authority. But you will receive power when the holy Spirit comes upon you, and you will be my witnesses in Jerusalem, throughout Judea and Samaria, and to the ends of the earth." When he had said this, as they were looking on, he was lifted up, and a cloud took him from their sight. While they were looking intently at the sky as he was going, suddenly two men dressed in white garments stood beside them. They said, "Men of Galilee, why are you standing there looking at the sky? This Jesus who has been taken up from you into heaven will return in the same way as you have seen him going into heaven." Then they returned to Jerusalem from the mount called Olivet, which is near Jerusalem, a sabbath day's journey away. Acts 1:6-12

> Then he led them [out] as far as Bethany, raised his hands, and blessed them. As he blessed them he parted from them and was taken up to heaven. They did him homage and then returned to Jerusalem with great joy, and they were continually in the temple praising God. Lk 24:50-53

Reflections

"... But you will receive power when the holy Spirit comes upon you,..." (Acts 1:8)

The work of establishing the church is clearly the operation of the Holy Spirit. Only after they were empowered by the Holy

Spirit were the apostles able to carry out their commission of evangelizing all nations. The same Holy Spirit is dynamic and operative in our lives if we are willing to be open and cooperative so that he can transform us into witnessing in our own locale.

Then he led them out as far as Bethany, . . . (Lk 24:50)
Be with Jesus and his disciples. As you walk along listen to the final instructions Jesus was giving them. His parting words must have been words of hope and encouragement, along with the reassurance that he would never leave them, but would be active in their lives. Once again he must have repeated his words spoken earlier: "I will come back again and take you to myself, so that where I am you also may be" (Jn 14:3).

They did him homage and then returned to Jerusalem with great joy, . . . (Lk 24:52)
Through the inspiration of the Holy Spirit, the disciples were beginning to understand the mystery of redemption and the glory which awaited them at his second coming. They were thrilled to be the messengers of this good news.

Moving Out of Prayer

Realizing that Jesus' public ministry is drawing to a close, you may wish to whisper repeatedly: "Thank you, Jesus; thank you, Jesus."

In your journal record how you feel. Does Jesus seem far away, or do you experience his risen and glorified presence with you?

Texts for Additional Days of Prayer

Colossians 3:1-4:	"Think of what is above, not of what is on earth." (v. 2)
Matthew 28:18-20:	". . . I am with you always, . . ." (v. 20)

Acts 1:13-14: "... All these devoted themselves with one accord to prayer, ..." (v. 14)

John 14:1-5: "... I will come back again ..." (v. 3)

John 14:15-21: "I will not leave you orphans; I will come to you." (v. 18)

TWENTY-EIGHT

Pentecost

*"And I will ask the Father,
and he will give you another Advocate
to be with you always."* **Jn 14:16**

Introduction

We are living in the Age of the Holy Spirit. Pope Leo XIII published an encyclical entitled *Divinum Illud* in 1897, which renewed much interest in the work of the Holy Spirit. The Second Vatican Council formally implemented the age of the Spirit. In the sixteen documents which the Council published, there are two hundred thirty-four mentions of the work of the Spirit.

The Holy Spirit is a unique personality. We can know him primarily through the gifts he gives and the fruits he produces within us. The inspired writers of sacred Scripture were unable to give us an understandable definition of the Third Person of the Blessed Trinity. They resorted to images and symbols. He is referred to as a breath, a gentle breeze, a mighty wind, fire, water, and the ever popular image of a dove. Translators of the codices of the Bible could not find adequate words to describe him. For this reason they often transliterated the Greek word Paraclete, which has a dual meaning. In a legal parlance, Paraclete means an advocate, or a defender. In non-legal language, it means a comforter, a consoler, a teacher.

The early Christians could not have given us a theological

definition of the Holy Spirit, but they certainly did experience him in their lives. Jesus said: "By their fruits you will know them" (Mt 7:20). Likewise we can know more about the Holy Spirit by the fruits he produces in us.

First, he is the Spirit of Love. He comes to fill us with his divine love. "The love of God has been poured out into our hearts through the Holy Spirit that has been given to us" (Rom 5:5). He helps us to love others when we know that we ourselves are loved.

The Holy Spirit teaches us how to pray. "In the same way, the Spirit too comes to the aid of our weakness; for we do not know how to pray as we ought, but the Spirit itself intercedes with inexpressible groanings" (Rom 8:26). The Holy Spirit seems to inundate our spirit and prays within us.

The Spirit helps us to take on the mind of Jesus. We are created in the image and likeness of God and are to become like him. Paul instructs us: "Have among yourselves the same attitude that is also yours in Christ Jesus" (Phil 2:5). In another place he urges us: "Be renewed in the spirit of your minds, and put on the new self, created in God's way in righteousness and holiness of truth" (Eph 4:23-24). We cannot really know the mind of Christ, nor succeed in becoming like him, unless the Spirit is at work within us. As we cooperate he will help us reach this goal in life.

The Holy Spirit is our teacher. He shows us how to teach a spiritual truth by witnessing to it in our own lives. "You will receive power when the holy Spirit comes upon you, and you will be my witnesses . . ." (Acts 1:8).

The Holy Spirit is our healer. "I will give you a new heart and place a new spirit within you . . . I will put my spirit within you . . ." (Ez 36:26-27). We need his healing daily to be able to reflect his love, peace, and joy to all we meet.

As the source of love, the Holy Spirit will assist us in building genuine Christian community. Community must be built on love not so much on laws, rules, and regulations.

"I, then, . . . urge you to live in a manner worthy of the call you have received, with all humility and gentleness, with patience, bearing with one another through love, striving to preserve the unity of the spirit through the bond of peace: one body and one

Spirit, as you were also called to the one hope of your call; one Lord, one faith, one baptism; one God and Father of all, who is over all and through all and in all." **Eph 4:1-6**

Scriptural Passage for Prayer

St. Luke's narrative (Acts 2) is considered the public outpouring of the Holy Spirit upon the infant church. There was one previous manifestation (Jn 20:22) and several subsequent manifestations: Samaria—Acts 8:14-17, Caesarea—Acts 10:44-48 and Ephesus—Acts 19:1-7.

Let your heart read between the lines as you listen to this account of the coming of the Holy Spirit on Pentecost:

When the time for Pentecost was fulfilled, they were all in one place together. And suddenly there came from the sky a noise like a strong driving wind, and it filled the entire house in which they were. Then there appeared to them tongues as of fire, which parted and came to rest on each one of them. And they were all filled with the holy Spirit and began to speak in different tongues, as the Spirit enabled them to proclaim.

Now there were devout Jews from every nation under heaven staying in Jerusalem. At this sound, they gathered in a large crowd, but they were confused because each one heard them speaking in his own language. They were astounded, and in amazement they asked, "Are not all these people who are speaking Galileans? Then how does each of us hear them in his own native language? We are Parthians, Medes, and Elamites, inhabitants of Mesopotamia, Judea and Cappadocia, Pontus and Asia, Phrygia and Pamphylia, Egypt and the districts of Libya near Cyrene, as well as travelers from Rome, both Jews and converts to Judaism, Cretans and Arabs, yet we hear them speaking in our own tongues of the mighty acts of God." They were all astounded and bewildered, and said to one another, "What does this mean?" But others said, scoffing, "They have had too much new wine." **Acts 2:1-13**

Reflections

And suddenly there came from the sky a noise like a strong driving wind, . . . (v. 2)
We have no clear-cut image of the Holy Spirit; hence there are various symbols used to describe his presence. A strong wind, in scriptural language, signifies the action of God, especially in the history of salvation.

Then there appeared to them tongues as of fire, which parted and came to rest on each one of them. (v. 3)
In the Old Testament fire symbolized the presence of God: the burning bush (Ex 3); the theophany on Mt. Sinai (Ex 19). Fire is one of the symbols used in referring to the Holy Spirit.

. . . they . . . began to speak in different tongues, as the Spirit enabled them to proclaim. (v. 4)
This might have been an ecstatic prayer language in praise of God commonly called today "praying in tongues." It might also have been a way to symbolize the worldwide mission of the church to preach the gospel to all nations.

Moving Out of Prayer

Spend a few moments being attentive to the Holy Spirit deep within you. Rest comfortably in this position as long as the Spirit motivates you.
Journal whatever reactions and feelings you experience.

Texts for Additional Days of Prayer

There is a profusion of references to the work of the Holy Spirit to be found in the New Testament. The following are only a few.

John 7:37-39: "He said this in reference to the Spirit. . . ." (v. 39)

John 14:16-17:	"But you know it, because [he] remains with you, and will be in you." (v. 17)
John 14:24-26:	"... he will teach you everything...." (v. 26)
John 16:12-14:	"... he will guide you to all truth...." (v. 13)
1 Corinthians 12:1-11:	"There are different kinds of spiritual gifts but the same Spirit; ..." (v. 4)
Galatians 5:22-23:	"In contrast, the fruit of the Spirit is love, joy, peace, ..." (v. 22)

TWENTY-NINE

Living With the Risen Jesus

"And behold, I am with you always, until the end of the age." **Mt 28:20**

Orientation

Jesus did not come into the world merely to show us the way to the Father, nor did he come only to redeem us by his death and resurrection and then return in glory to the Father. No, Jesus came to live with us in his risen, glorified life. Did he not say: "I will not leave you orphans; I will come to you" (Jn 14:18)?

One of the most comforting and consoling truths in our whole deposit of faith is the mystery of God's indwelling within us. The risen Jesus is living with us and within us. It is a mysterious kind of indwelling which we are not able to comprehend or fathom. We need to remind ourselves constantly of his abiding presence.

We are never alone. Jesus is always with us, more a part of us than the blood circulating throughout our body, more a part of us than the oxygen we inhale twenty-five thousand times each day. In fact, our spirit is living within his Spirit. We are completely enveloped by the Holy Spirit. "In him we live and move and have our being" (Acts 17:28).

Baptism. Just as the resurrection of Jesus is the greatest feast in the church's calendar, so our Baptism is one of the greatest events in our own lives. At the moment of our Baptism, the resurrection becomes personalized. The risen Jesus comes to make his dwelling place with us.

In Baptism we become members of God's family. The Father adopts us as his sons and daughters. He shares with us the greatest of all his gifts—his own divine life in the person of Jesus through the power of the Holy Spirit. The Spirit is the fullness of Jesus living within us.

When we were baptized we became the temples of the Holy Spirit as St. Paul reminds us on several occasions. He asks: "Do you not know that you are the temple of God, and the Spirit of God dwells in you?" (1 Cor 3:16). A little later in the same letter he asks the question again: "Do you not know that your body is a temple of the holy Spirit within you . . .?" (1 Cor 6:19).

The Holy Spirit's indwelling is by no means a static presence. On the contrary, he is dynamic and operative within us— empowering us to live our baptismal commitment more fully each day. This awareness enabled St. Paul to say: "I live, no longer I, but Christ lives in me" (Gal 2:20).

Body of Christ. Jesus lives not only in us, but in all of our brothers and sisters throughout the world. The church is the body of Christ. Jesus is dwelling in all the members of the church. He is one with the church. This, too, is a mystery.

We cannot love the Lord without loving others. In fact, we love God through our brothers and sisters. This is what Jesus meant when he said: "Amen, I say to you, whatever you did for one of these least brothers of mine, you did for me" (Mt 25:40). Jesus did not say that he would consider it as being done for him, but that we are actually doing for him since he dwells within even his least brothers.

Scriptural Passage for Prayer

Jesus was a teacher par excellence. He knew that our finite minds could not grasp this unique mystery of his indwelling. For this reason, in a brief but picturesque allegory, he explains this mysterious indwelling:

"I am the true vine, and my Father is the vine grower. He takes away every branch in me that does not bear fruit, and everyone that does he prunes so that it bears more fruit. You are already pruned because of the word that I spoke to you. Remain in me, as I remain in you. Just as a branch cannot bear fruit on its own unless it remains on the vine, so neither can you unless you remain in me. I am the vine, you are the branches. Whoever remains in me and I in him will bear much fruit, because without me you can do nothing. Anyone who does not remain in me will be thrown out like a branch and wither; people will gather them and throw them into a fire and they will be burned. If you remain in me and my words remain in you, ask for whatever you want and it will be done for you. By this is my Father glorified, that you bear much fruit and become my disciples."

Jn 15:1-8

Reflections

There are a number of resting places in this brief allegory. We will highlight only a few. Let the Spirit lead you to what he wants you to hear.

"I am the true vine, . . ." (v. 1)
Without the vine a branch cannot possibly survive. Jesus is the source of divine life in us, nourishing us, enabling us to produce fruit.

". . . and everyone that does he prunes so that it bears more fruit." (v. 2)
Note that Jesus does not imply that we are not bearing fruit, but we must be pruned to bear even more fruit. This is the conditioning process which is going on within us at all times. Pruning may be painful at times, but it is essential for the vine to produce abundantly. Likewise we must be pruned of undue attachments to become a fruit-producing disciple.

"You are already pruned because of the word that I spoke to you." (v. 3)
The Word of God has a tremendous transforming power to turn us away from worldly concerns and help us to focus on him. As we pray with his Word, this conversion may go on within us without our even being aware of it.

"Remain in me, as I remain in you. . . ." (v. 4)
We can separate ourselves from Jesus by sin. In this state we will produce no fruit. However, Jesus meant even more. The more we keep ourselves aware of his abiding presence, the better will he be able to produce fruit through us.

". . . without me you can do nothing." (v. 5)
We are well aware of this truth, but we forget so readily and want to take over ourselves. Jesus is also saying that with him we can do all things. Even with a casual knowledge of a grape vine, we know that the sweetness and richness of the grapes depends on their exposure to the sun. Jesus is the sun and our exposure to him will determine the richness of the harvest we produce.

"By this is my Father glorified, that you bear much fruit . . ." (v. 8)
Think of our everyday duties and demands performed out of love. With Jesus give honor and glory to the transcendent God of heaven and earth.

Moving Out of Prayer

Visit with Jesus dwelling within you and express the sentiments of your heart. Ask him to keep you more aware of his abiding presence.

In your journal record whatever the Spirit urges you to write.

Texts for Additional Days of Prayer

Here are some reminders of our living in Jesus and Jesus living in us:

Galatians 3:27:	"For all of you who were baptized into Christ have clothed yourselves with Christ."
Colossians 2:6-7:	"So, as you received Christ Jesus the Lord, walk in him, rooted in him and

	built upon him and established in the faith as you were taught, abounding in thanksgiving."
John 15:4:	"Remain in me, as I remain in you. . . ."
Ephesians 3:14-19:	". . . and that Christ may dwell in your hearts through faith, . . ." (v. 17)
1 Peter 1:3-9:	". . . Who in his great mercy gave us a new birth to a living hope through the resurrection of Jesus Christ from the dead, . . ." (v. 3)

THIRTY

Finding God in All Things

When you look for me, you will find me.
Yes, when you seek me with all your heart,
you will find me with you, . . . **Jer 29:13-14**

Introduction

The themes presented in this chapter embrace the whole of salvation history. Their fourfold dimension enables us to recall the four stages of God's evolving plan for our salvation. It would not be conducive to our prayer to focus on more than one stage at a time. Each separate stage is sufficient for one or more prayer periods.

We are a people who love and enjoy celebrations. We need only a minor reason to call for a celebration. However, we cannot have a genuine celebration without a memorial. We celebrate Christmas to recall that God so loved us that he gave us his only Son. On Thanksgiving Day, we pause to express our thanks and appreciation for all the blessings the Lord has showered upon us. The same is true of the many celebrations which we hold throughout our lives.

To remember is to be grateful. It is also true that a grateful person is a prayerful person.

Salvation History. In this prayer time, we want to find God in all the stages of salvation. As we reflect on the history of salvation, we will discover how personal and intricate is God's plan to help us grow and mature in our personal relationship with him. He planned the most minute details of our lives, even though we were not aware of it at the time. Someday we will understand how all the happenings of our life fit together like the pieces of a puzzle to form a perfect picture.

Be with God—Father, Son, and Holy Spirit—and let him review with you all that he did and will continue to do for you. Let us reflect on four different areas of his plan for our salvation. These four stages of salvation history are renewed for us each year by the church in her liturgical cycle. During Advent we recall the promises and prophecies of the Old Testament leading up to the incarnation. Immediately after the nativity we relive with Jesus his public ministry. Lent is the ideal time to remember the passion and death of our Savior. The rest of the year we rejoice with the resurrected Jesus and the Holy Spirit in his work of sanctification.

Creation

Orientation. Creation is an expression of love. It is providing for the person we love. God created everything to meet our needs and for our appreciation.

Recall all the blessings and benefits in the order of creation and grace which God has conferred upon you throughout your lifetime. Go over your life year by year and review the people, places, and experiences you have enjoyed.

Recount the many works of creation which are God's personal gift to you: your eyes, hands, parents, and friends—to name but a few. St. Paul asks: "What do you possess that you have not received?" (1 Cor 4:7). Rest with whatever touches your heart and share it with the Lord.

Scriptural Passages for Prayer. The inspired Word of the Lord recorded in Scripture may help you enter into listening prayer. Here are starting points to consider:

Genesis 1:1-31: "God looked at everything he had made, and he found it very good...." (v. 31)

Psalm 104:	A lyrical account of the seven stages of creation extolling the beauty and goodness of God.
Psalm 148:	A hymn praising and glorifying our Almighty Creator.

Incarnation

Orientation. When sin entered the world, it severed our love relationship with our Father. God did not abandon us, as well he might. His love prevailed. He promised and sent us a Redeemer in the Person of Jesus. "For God so loved the world that he gave his only Son, so that everyone who believes in him might not perish but might have eternal life" (Jn 3:16).

Jesus came into the world to reveal the infinite love which the Father has for each one of us personally and individually.

Jesus brought us hope and promise. He came to teach us a way of life which would lead us to eternal salvation. Throughout his public ministry he taught us by word. He could explain a profound mystery by parable or illustration taken from everyday life. He set forth some standards for living his way of life such as the beatitudes.

Even more important he lived every truth he taught. His own lifestyle is an example and inspiration to us. He challenged us to follow his example: "I give you a new commandment: love one another. As I have loved you, so you also should love one another" (Jn 13:34).

St. Gregory the Great expressed a truism in these words: "When one practices first and preaches afterwards, one is really teaching with power." A modern dictum states the same truth in these words: "We must not only talk the talk, but we must walk the walk."

Jesus did not simply give us the norms for our Christian living and then depart into his glory. Through his risen, exalted life he lives with us and within us to inspire and motivate us, to encourage and strengthen us, to support and guide us.

Scriptural Passages for Prayer. Listening to his Word will assist us in living his way of life.

Matthew 11:28-30:	"Come to me, all you who labor and are burdened and I will give you rest." (v. 28)
Luke 9:23-27:	... "If anyone wishes to come after me, he must deny himself and take up his cross daily and follow me." (v. 23)
Matthew 5:3-12:	"Blessed are the poor in spirit, ... they who mourn, ..." (vv. 3-4)

Redemption

Orientation. Sin is a refusal to love. Sin is a refusal to respond to the outpouring of God's love by willfully insisting on doing our own selfish will. When we love a person we want to do what pleases that person most. Love forgets self in order to do something for the person loved. Sin entered the world because mankind refused to respond to God's love.

Jesus came into the world to offer the Father an infinite act of love by offering his very life for our redemption. His total act of unselfish love restored the bond which humanity had severed by its refusal to love and obey the will of the Lord.

Jesus taught us that if we truly love God, we will naturally try to avoid sin to the best of our ability. Jesus offered everything he did from Bethlehem to Calvary, from the crib to the cross, as a love-offering. He urges us to make a similar commitment in love.

Scriptural Passages for Prayer. Jesus loves us so much that he willingly laid down his life to redeem us. He tells us of his sacrificial love:

John 10:1-18:	"... I lay down my life in order to take it up again. No one takes it from me, ..." (vv. 17-18)
Ephesians 2:1-10:	"But God, who is rich in mercy, because of the great love he had for us, even

	when we were dead in our transgressions, brought us to life with Christ..." (v. 5)
Philippians 2:5-11:	"Have among yourselves the same attitude that is also yours in Christ Jesus." (v. 5)

Resurrection

Orientation. One of the many fruits of the redemption is our potential to be filled with the divine life and love which Jesus came to give us. By rising from the dead, Jesus was able to share his risen, exalted life with us. He is living with us and within us.

The resurrection put the seal of approval on all that Jesus did and taught. He fulfilled every prophecy and promise which was made about him.

Jesus also rose from the dead because he loves us and wants to be united with us. We want to be close to the people we love. Jesus could not separate himself from us because of his boundless love for us. What a unique dignity is ours!

Scriptural Passages for Prayer. In our prayer, let us ponder this divine gift and may our hearts overflow with gratitude and love.

John 15:1-8:	"I am the true vine and my Father is the vine grower." (v. 1)
Romans 6:1-23:	"... just as Christ was raised from the dead by the glory of the Father, we too might live in newness of life." (v. 4)
Romans 8:14-39:	"... but you received a spirit of adoption, through which we cry, *Abba,* 'Father!'" (v. 15)

Reflections

As we spend quality time in prayer we will find God's plans for our salvation unfolding in these four stages for our spiritual growth and maturation. We will be granted awe-inspiring insights stirring our hearts to respond in love, peace, joy, and gratitude to the God who overwhelms us with his creating, providing, forgiving, enduring, and saving love.

Moving Out of Prayer

Let your heart quietly sing the praises of our gracious Father who created us, our loving Jesus who redeemed us, and the Holy Spirit who sanctifies us.

Note in your journal whatever your heart prompts you.

Texts for Additional Days of Prayer

For each additional day of prayer on these themes of salvation, return to the Scriptures already suggested and select one for further prayer. Spend a full day on each theme in sequence. You could go through the four themes twice for a total of eight additional days of prayer.

www.ingramcontent.com/pod-product-compliance
Lightning Source LLC
Chambersburg PA
CBHW060608230426
43670CB00011B/2017